Face the Music

Face the Music

MY STORY

ALFIE BOE

With Terry Ronald

**EBURY
SPOTLIGHT**

2

Ebury Spotlight, an imprint of Ebury Publishing
20 Vauxhall Bridge Road
London SW1V 2SA

Ebury Spotlight is part of the Penguin Random House group of companies
whose addresses can be found at global.penguinrandomhouse.com

First published by Ebury Spotlight in 2023

www.penguin.co.uk

A CIP catalogue record for this book is available from the British Library

ISBN 9781529910346

Printed and bound in Great Britain by Clays Ltd, Elcograf S.p.A.

The authorised representative in the EEA is Penguin Random House Ireland,
Morrison Chambers, 32 Nassau Street, Dublin D02 YH68

Penguin Random House is committed to a sustainable future
for our business, our readers and our planet. This book is made
from Forest Stewardship Council® certified paper.

In the final stages of your life, mum, you still try to guide me and teach me as best you can. I hope this book is a reflection of that, and the happiness I'm trying to bring to others through my memories, teaching and life challenges that you taught me to cope with and learn from.

I love you mum.

CONTENTS

CHAPTER 1

UNDER ICE

I'm at the edge now. Waiting. The first one to go, but maybe that's better. Get it over with. Get it done. I mean, it's sub-zero temperatures and I'm in my shorts. Just my shorts. It's OK, though; I want to do this. I'm ready.

High in the Italian Alps, I'm surrounded by snow, the most spectacular mountains, and ... a camera crew. Goggles on, rubbing my hands together, I'm about to jump into a hole that's been carved out of the ice and swim underneath it. On television.

Almost without realising, I'm plunging downwards, breaking the surface: feet, chest, shoulders. Up to my neck in freezing water. The shock of it takes hold fast, but I breathe like I've been shown by the show's expert, Wim Hof, slow and deep, almost like meditating. Eventually, it's bearable. Still biting but not eating through me. Now it's exhilarating, energising. I'm part of it rather than fighting against it.

Push downwards once you're in. That's what I was told. Really push down, just to get underneath the ice, because it's ten inches thick, he said, maybe twelve.

OK, Alfie, take a breath. A good, deep breath.

I'm submerged now, but not far enough. My head smacks against the edge of the opening in the ice, and it hurts. Not the start I was hoping for. *You need to go further down.* I push myself down again, this time with more force. Then I find the line I must grab hold of to help pull me through. *OK, let's do this. Let's swim under ice.*

I'm away now, pushing through the darkness, gripping the line, kicking my feet. It doesn't seem long before I'm firing myself back towards the light above me, rising up through the opening, breath bursting out of my lungs and into the air. I feel exhilaration, a sense of achievement. I've swum under the ice. But this is just the first hole, halfway along. It's an even longer swim to reach the second opening – the final one. This time it's double the length.

Down I go again, further down this time. No more headbanging (I'll save that for rock concerts). Find the line, grip the line, pull myself along the line. Nothing but black water, except for a camera light that looks like it could be coming from a mile away.

I'm moving faster now, swimming through with ease, but then I feel the urge to slow down. Consciously. I want it all to last, to sense my surroundings and commit it all to memory.

The solitude I feel looking down at the black water below me makes me realise how alone I am, how alone I've been, while above, there's this crystal-like shimmer. Sunlight, filtering through the ice like . . . diamonds. Wim was right; it does look like diamonds. It really does.

Forward now, faster because at some point soon, I need to breathe. Then something occurs to me. This isn't just physical endurance. In fact, for me, it's not really about the body at all. Swimming under this ice, pulling myself through this freezing water, I'm in control of my mind, my emotions, and my feelings. And it's the first time I've felt that way in . . . I can't even think how long. Too long. Without any control.

It's a powerful moment, shedding the bad stuff, letting it sink into the blackness, then looking up at the underside of the ice, seeing how clear and fresh and bright it is above me. That's where I want to go; that's where I need to head.

As I finally come out from under, I'm feeling proud, excited even. But more than that, there's a sense of calm, like a weight has been lifted. The realisation that I've gone the distance and at the same time addressed my biggest fear overwhelms me. Not the fear of diving into freezing cold water and swimming under ice; that wasn't it. What scared me the most for so long was the idea that I'd be stuck living with my mistakes forever. That I'd never be able to move on. Now, as I pull myself up and out of the water, I realise something in me has shifted and changed. I'd gone under the ice one person and come out another.

CHAPTER 2

LIVING IN THE CLOUDS

Our house in Salt Lake City was the perfect home for a growing family: my wife Sarah and me; our children, Grace and Alfie; and our pets, a golden retriever called Guinness and our two cats, Arthur and Alice.

It was a detached house in a neighbourhood called the Upper Avenues, with a little swimming pool in the back garden, which the kids loved jumping in and out of on warm summer days, and we were thirty minutes down the canyon from the ski resorts.

Salt Lake City is the capital of Utah, sitting on the Jordan River at the south-eastern end of the Great Salt Lake. It's set against a backdrop of mountains, which frame the skyline magnificently. But besides all the wild beauty of the state, the city itself is a lively urban and cultural centre with lots going on. Most weekends, we'd either ski or go to pop and rock concert tours that came to the city during the summer. Sometimes, though, I would simply take off and hike with Sarah and the children or ride my motorbike around the hills.

From the front, our house looked like a fairly modern structure but with a traditional-looking facade. There was a driveway, steps leading to the front door, and a small rose garden. The house also boasted a wraparound balcony. The best thing about it, though, was the view from the back. As you walked through the house, it hit you. A stunning outlook over the whole of Salt Lake Valley, a sprawling panorama which is surrounded by steep mountains in almost every direction.

From there, we could see the sunrises and the storms rolling in. When there was an inversion (where cold air is trapped beneath warm air) we could look down onto a blanket of cloud that sat in the base of the valley covering the whole of the city, so only the tops of the skyscrapers were visible. On some mornings, sipping my coffee on the balcony, I'd look down on it, feeling like we were living above the clouds. Bright sunshine above; grey and misty below.

Whenever we got hit by snow, we really got hit. The weird thing about Utah is it seems to snow on cue. You can almost guarantee that right after Thanksgiving, you get a huge dump of snow, which will gradually melt away, ready for the Christmas snow. There was usually a generous fall of snow at Christmas – a long, deep blanket of it. We woke up one Christmas morning to find snow halfway up the outside wall of the house. You could literally fall into it and completely disappear; it was that deep.

Extreme weather aside, it was a lovely existence. Idyllic, you might say.

Despite Sarah being the American in the family, she wasn't the one who had wanted to settle in America in 2013; it was me. I somehow felt like I hadn't ticked all the boxes yet. I hadn't explored all the possibilities of what I could do there.

I think deep down I still had the vision of America that I'd had as a kid, seeing images of it on television and in the movies and, of course, listening to the music. When I was growing up in 1970s Fleetwood, Lancashire, my dad, Alfie, was a bit of a ballroom dancer – not by profession; he worked for ICI as a process worker making chlorine gas – but he loved his dancing. Consequently, he played a lot of American swing and big band records when I was little: Glenn Miller and Syd Lawrence. Whenever Mum and Dad threw a party at home, which was something they did throughout their lives together, it would be those records that went on the record player first.

In my younger days, you'd probably find me complaining about the music selection, wondering when Dad was going to throw on something a bit more rock 'n' roll, something I could sing and dance along to. But the older I got, the more I started to appreciate the music my dad played. These days, when I play those records, it's like a treasure trove of memories of my dad. I love to hear them because they remind me so much of him.

As far as the movies went, I loved the forties and fifties classics as a child: cowboy films with stars like John Wayne and Clint Eastwood. I also loved Elvis – his music, live performances, and his movies. A favourite of mine was *Flaming Star*, a western set on the Texas frontier. *G.I Blues* was another, and, of course, I had the soundtrack albums. Elvis has always been a huge influence on me. Initially, because his voice was so powerful and distinctive, and he's such a dynamic performer. But the thing that really drew me to him was his great sense of humour – on stage and during interviews. He always seemed to be laughing and making light of situations. I think that's really informed the way I am with my audiences. My approach is always, let's not take things too seriously; let's have a good time. It's important to me, especially because some of the music I perform can be fairly serious. It's nice to put people at ease. I want the people who might be coming to a classical concert for the first time to know that they can relax and have fun. It doesn't have to be stuffy!

When I started playing the drums, around the age of eleven or twelve, it was American jazz drummer Gene Krupa who inspired me, and I'd listen to recordings of him over and over again. It was the 1980s, but when I looked for a grounding in rock 'n' roll music, it was 1950s artists like The Big Bopper, Buddy Holly, The Beach Boys, The Everly Brothers and many more. True, most of these artists were a bit before my time, but I was the youngest of nine (three brothers and five sisters), and having lots of older siblings meant that I grew up with some of their tastes and interests bleeding into mine. Plus, as a budding drummer, songs like 'Wipe Out' by The Surfaris and some of The Beach Boys' singles were my absolute go-to records.

As a kid, I'd fly up and down Fleetwood Beach on my bike with headphones on, listening to The Beach Boys. OK, so it wasn't exactly a convertible T-Bird in sun-drenched California, but it was good enough for me. If only I'd known back then that I would one day be on the same bill as The Beach Boys. But that story I'll tell later.

In my teenage years, rock 'n' roll 'big hair' bands became the thing; American bands like Guns N' Roses and Bon Jovi were always top of my playlist. Again, it was all about massive high-energy performances, and I loved it. Of course, I was into some of the UK rock bands as well: Iron Maiden, Def Leppard, and Queen. To be perfectly honest, given my musical tastes growing up, it's a bit of a surprise I ever became an opera singer. Saying that, I guess there is equal drama in both genres. Sometimes, the energy and emotion in a rock power ballad accompanied by a huge bank of strings and horns has all the extravagance and spectacle of an opera.

Back when I was young then, America always looked like a really cool place, and I wanted to be part of it.

When I got older and got my first big break in America, the chance to work on Broadway, it held a different sort of magic. That was when all sorts of doors opened up for me.

It was 2002, and I'd just finished a seven-month run performing in Baz Luhrmann's *La Bohème* on Broadway. We'd started the show in San Francisco, then, after Broadway, we took it to LA for a three-month run. While we were there, we had every movie star under the sun come to see the show – because of Baz's name, of course. One evening, Danny DeVito and Rhea Perlman came to watch the show. I really wanted to meet them, so the company manager invited them backstage to say hi to the cast after the show. Danny seemed like such a great, down-to-earth bloke, and Rhea was lovely.

As we walked back to our cars later that night, Danny asked me how I was enjoying LA, and what I was up to next.

'I'd like to get into film and television,' I said.

Isn't that what you do when in Hollywood? You go to castings and auditions; you get your foot in the door.

'OK, well, I could introduce you to my agent, Fred Specktor,' Danny said. 'He's vice president at CAA.'

'That would be great,' I said.

Fred is a legendary Hollywood agent, and CAA represented some of the biggest talents in Hollywood, so I was more than grateful for the introduction. I invited Fred to come to see me in the show and then met him at his office in Beverly Hills. After that, Fred set up meetings with every casting director in LA at all the movie studios. I did the rounds, going for meetings at 20th Century Fox, Paramount, Warner Brothers, and even Steven Spielberg's company, DreamWorks.

The usual takeaway was someone telling me, with a fake smile and singsong accent, 'We can't think of anything now, but keep an eye on what's coming out, and if there's anything that you think is suitable for you, come in and have a read.'

Those meetings never came to much, but I knew it was still all out there, ready for the taking if I put my mind to it. I suppose that's why I wasn't done with America; I still wanted to be successful there and achieve more.

We didn't move straight to our lovely house in Salt Lake City, however. After we packed up our home in Woodstock, Oxfordshire, we landed first in LA, where I got back in touch with Fred to discuss what new opportunities there might be for work, and he set up some more meetings

Having just arrived and with no fixed abode, we ended up staying with a relation of Sarah's in Santa Monica, while looking for a place of our own. But Sarah didn't feel comfortable in LA. We were a nine-hour drive from Salt Lake City, her home, and LA just didn't feel like the right environment for her.

I shouldn't have been surprised; this was a pretty big change for all of us. We'd just left a lovely family home in a village in the Cotswolds, and suddenly we were living in a spare room in her mum's cousin's house in Santa Monica. It was quite an upheaval, especially with our young daughter, Grace, and one-year-old Alfie.

At the time, I was also recording my eighth studio album, *Trust*, with some legendary American musicians: Jay Bellerose, Leland Sklar, and the great Booker T. Jones on Hammond organ. To be honest, I quite liked being in LA, and felt like I was getting into the swing of being there. Sarah felt differently.

'I don't think I can settle here, Alfie,' she told me. 'I don't think I can envisage putting the kids through school in LA.'

It's funny, we came very close to buying a house up a canyon near Malibu, LA, but the survey said it was home to a colony of termites. Looking back, it wasn't the right house for us anyway; we probably wouldn't have stayed there for long. For a start, Sarah would have been very isolated when I wasn't around. Maybe the termite infestation was fate trying to tell us something. In the end we decided to pack up the car and drive the nine hours to Salt Lake City, where we moved into Sarah's dad's apartment. Eventually, after a couple of months of searching for the perfect property, we bought our beautiful house on the hill.

•   •   •

I guess you could say we were fairly nomadic as a family, as this was actually our second stint living in Salt Lake City. We first moved out there in 2009 and stayed for a couple of years before moving to west London and then to the Cotswolds.

In fact, Salt Lake City was where Alfie was born. I was in the midst of a UK tour at the time, and Sarah was heavily pregnant – expecting any day. I'd been performing around the UK until just before Christmas, and was due back in the UK for my next concert on 20 January. The last thing we wanted was for Alfie to be born one day, then me packing my bags and leaving the next, so we decided that Sarah would have an induced labour. She would hopefully give birth on 1 January, giving me time to spend with her and my newborn son before heading back to England. It might sound a bit odd to schedule the birth of a child around my work, but that's the life of a travelling entertainer for you.

We turned up at the hospital on the morning of New Year's Day with Sarah looking radiant. Once things were set in motion, there were a few hours of waiting around, so I decided to pop out and get something to eat. Inevitably, I chose exactly the wrong time. Just as I took possession of a sad-looking burrito in the hospital canteen, I got a phone call from the midwife.

'Alfie, you've got to come back to the ward. Sarah's starting.'

I hot-footed it back up to the room – I can't remember if the burrito came with – and arrived just as Sarah was about to give birth. I stepped into the room.

'So, Alfie, what sort of role do you want to have in this birth?' asked Dr Yamashiro, our wonderful consultant.

'Well, doctor, I want to be here with Sarah,' I said. 'I want to hold her hand, make sure she feels safe and secure, and give her as much support as I possibly can.'

'Right, well, you're going to be doing a little bit more than that,' he said.

'Really?'

'Yes, Alfie. You're going to deliver this baby.'

'No, man.' I laughed nervously.

'Yes,' he nodded. 'You're going to help Sarah bring your baby into the world. I'll be right by you and tell you exactly what to do, but you're going to do it.'

Before I knew it, I was putting on green scrubs, gloves and a mask, not really knowing what was expected of me.

While Sarah was pushing with the contractions – doing all the hard work – she looked at me and said, 'Are you OK? You look like you're going to faint.'

'If you're going to faint, do it away from the table,' the midwife added.

In between telling Sarah when to push, Dr Yamashiro started to give me instructions.

'When you see his head crown, put your hand on top of it because he will fly out!'

'Are you serious? Fly out?'

By this time, I was full of adrenaline; it was a real mix of nerves and excitement. Then I watched as my son's head appeared, and did as the doctor had told me.

'Now make sure you hold his head while I check the umbilical cord isn't around his neck. Then, on this next contraction, when his shoulders are out, I want you to put your hand underneath his back, lift him and put him on top of Sarah's chest.'

When the contraction came, I was taken aback by the force of his little head beneath my hand. Meanwhile, Sarah pushed and pushed as his shoulders, then his waist came out. Just as the doctor had instructed me, I lifted him out, picked him up and placed him on Sarah. I could hardly believe what had just happened. I had helped bring my son into the world. Alfred Robert, after my dad. I'd delivered him – with the help of an expert! It was an incredible moment.

Sarah spent a couple of nights in the hospital before we put little Alfie in the car and took him back home. I loved those first days I spent with my new little boy, and when I had to go back on tour in the UK, it was a wrench having to leave him so soon.

CHAPTER 3

PUSHING MYSELF

Living in Utah, thirty minutes from the ski resorts, meant that skiing was simply part of life. It wasn't so much like going on a skiing holiday; it was almost part of our daily routine. Having grown up in the area, Sarah was an excellent skier, so she taught me how to ski while we lived there. I have to admit, I found it bloody tricky. That said, I was perhaps slightly overconfident the first time I ever tried it.

'I'll take to this no problem,' I told everyone, thinking I'd be a natural.

That was probably why nobody went for easy options when teaching me to ski. I was thrown down some Blue Squares – intermediate runs, with a slope of 25–40 per cent – which seemed steep to me, and at least one Black Diamond, which was like skiing off a cliff. I mean, you start doing those sorts of runs when you've been skiing for a good amount of time, not right off the bat. Not on your first couple of goes.

That first day, despite my confidence and bravado, I realised I couldn't really ski at all. Great. I also couldn't stop when I needed to. What I was quite good at was falling down, and, given that I couldn't turn left or stop, I was also fairly adept at crashing into things. Well, you have to be good at something.

So, let's just say it was a little daunting throwing myself head-first down a mountain on a couple of planks of wood. (Especially at a time when the rules about wearing helmets were a bit more relaxed, and my only real protection from a potential head injury was a stripy bobble hat.)

On another of my early skiing adventures, we were at a ski resort called Snowbird, which is in the Wasatch Range of the Rocky Mountains near Salt Lake City. On the way up this beast of a mountain, riding on a ski lift called Little Cloud, I noticed a little sign below me. It said something like, do not ride this lift if you are not an expert skier. I thought, *I'm on the bloody lift now, it's a little late in the day to tell me that!* True to form, that day I ended up crashing into a tree and someone had to help dig me out of the snow.

Still, despite the mishaps, the après-ski was always good. It was often getting back on skis afterwards that was a problem!

I persevered with it, and, like anything, the more you do it, the more confident you get. Gradually I got the hang of it, and once I did, we skied every season. My kids are great skiers. In Utah, they pretty much grow up with skis on their feet, so once they can walk, they're skiing. When Grace was very little, we'd wrap her up warm, put her on a sledge and take her cross-country skiing. There were times when we'd hit a ditch, and she would roll off into the snow and disappear, and we had to run and dig her out.

• • •

Another thing that we loved to do at home in Salt Lake City was to entertain. And boy, did we have parties! So many parties at the house, where we'd invite all our friends over and cook like crazy – proper big feasts and celebrations. I enjoy a bit of a theme to an evening, and that included the music. If we were having a St Patrick's Day party, I'd put on some Irish music. If I was cooking Italian food for my guests, I put on some Italian opera. I also liked American folk and Americana, which was always the perfect soundtrack for where we lived. And, of course, a sprinkling of classic rock – always! I guess you could say it was a bit of anything and everything (like my career!)

Sarah and I were always able to throw a good party, to bring people together and celebrate each other. One of the biggest I remember was my fortieth birthday, in 2013, which we celebrated at home. Well, I say remember. I'm not sure how much of it I actually do remember. The night ended with me jumping off the first-floor balcony into the swimming pool, fully clothed, with a giant, Vegas-style pimp chalice in my hand. Classy, right?

The party theme was the 1970s (since I was born in '73),

so everyone turned up in seventies clothes and wigs. I was wearing white boots with zips at the side, hideous beige polyester pants, a satin shirt unbuttoned to the navel, and 1970s-era Elvis glasses. Sarah found a lot of the seventies stuff in thrift stores, I believe – or maybe in the back of my wardrobe. We had a disco downstairs, caterers who made my favourite barbecue food and a well-stocked bar, fully serviced. This, of course, was all organised by Sarah. She was amazing at doing that sort of thing.

I remember being so happy and high on life that day. Surrounded by family and friends while the music played and lights flashed. I mean, why wouldn't you jump into a swimming pool fully clothed? We all ended up partying into the early hours and the house was inevitably an absolute mess the next day. I felt as rough as hell, but it had been well worth it.

Not all birthday plans were as successful as my fortieth, though. One year, for Grace's birthday, I decided I'd make her the best birthday cake ever.

On the morning of her birthday, I got up early and grilled some sardines on toast for my breakfast – not everyone's idea of a delicious breakfast, I know – and then set about baking the sponge for the cake. The thing is, I baked the bloody sponge in the same oven that I'd grilled the sardines in, so the sponge just soaked up the pungent smell. Poor Grace ended up with this beautiful-looking chocolate birthday cake that tasted of fish. She still hasn't let me forget it.

'Remember when you made me a sardine cake for my birthday, Dad?'

'It's a European thing, Grace – I was trying to start a trend.'

• • •

We did a lot of family trips to Idaho back then; it's about four hours' drive from Salt Lake. Sarah's family had a cabin, owned by her grandma, and we went there every summer. It was a gorgeous spot: a peaceful getaway from the world where you could barely get a phone signal. A 1930s-style log cabin in the middle of nowhere, surrounded by forests and fields, with a peaceful, idyllic river behind it. Perfect for connecting with nature, getting into the woodland and rivers, hiking or trekking in the Idaho hills or the Sawtooth Range of mountains. Twenty minutes' drive away, there was a pair of lovely towns called Sun Valley and Ketchum. They are beautiful, dusty, rustic old mountain towns, and visiting them feels like stepping back into the fifties.

I loved to eat outdoors at the cabin. We'd grill some good steaks on the barbecue, have a beer or two, and light a campfire where we'd sit looking at the stars and listening to the wildlife. It was a complete escape from the madness that was my world at the time – a complete departure from all the touring and recording. We even went once in the middle of winter when the place was usually all locked up. I remember carrying Grace from the car, wrapped up in a papoose, all warm and cosy. You can't really stay overnight in winter because it's way too cold, and we virtually had to dig our way in because the snow was so deep. Once inside, I did my best to light a fire and then made some soup to warm everyone up. At one point, I spilt some of the soup on the kitchen counter, and it immediately froze – that's how cold it was!

I suppose you could say that the cabin was where Sarah and I were officially engaged. I'd proposed to her back in New York in 2002 while I was on Broadway doing *La Bohème*. It was actually quite stressful. I'd got the ring, all ready to propose, but there I was, walking around Manhattan, desperately trying to book a restaurant to pop the question. Not having planned far enough ahead, all the restaurants I wanted to go to were either full or closed for refurbishment. Green Room, Greenwich Kitchen, Rockefeller – I couldn't get a reservation anywhere. Eventually, I bumped into a friend of mine, Alvaro Domingo – son of Plácido – and we went for a beer. I filled him in on my fruitless quest for a proposal spot.

'Hey, my father has a restaurant called Pampano on East 49th Street – beautiful Mexican seafood', he said. 'Why don't I book you a table, and you can go there tonight?'

I told Sarah we were going out for a burger and fries, although with me done up in a suit, I'm not sure how convincing that was.

'Why on earth are you wearing a suit to go for a burger?' she asked.

Still, it all worked out, and that night I got down on one knee.

When I asked her dad's permission at the family cabin a short time later, and he agreed, it was official. Just another reason why the cabin was a special place for us. Idyllic in every way.

For me, that family time was special. Despite living in America, so much of my work was back in the UK, and there would be long stretches of time when I'd be away, which I knew was hard for Sarah – especially with two young children. I always felt like I had to make the most of it. Looking back, I sometimes wonder if I did.

•   •   •

Sarah had an uncle in Idaho, Pierre, who was a lovely guy, about ten years older than me. He and I hit it off right away; immediate friends and, in some ways, immediate brothers. We spoke often, connected through our love of music. Pierre was a big rocker, and a fellow huge Rolling Stones fan. I guess he was the epitome of what I imagined a cowboy to be. He spoke with a real western drawl and had the whole authentic cowboy vibe going on. He rode horses and motorbikes, skied fast, drove his cars fast, and liked to live life on the edge.

I suppose you could say Pierre fitted my childhood idea of the heroes I saw in movies as a kid, wanting to live that American adventure. He had this devil-may-care approach to life that lit something in me, although that side of him sometimes masked what was going on behind.

As wild as he appeared, though, he was one of the calmest, most peaceful, loving guys I'd ever met. Tall and slim with small facial features, he had a twinkle in his eyes and a wry little smile that always seemed to sit at the corner of his mouth. Pierre had a great sense of humour; he was always laughing, and, like me, he adored rock 'n' roll music. Watching him play air guitar to The Rolling Stones' 'Sympathy for the Devil' is a memory that will stay with me forever. He had the Keith Richards guitar stance and the Jagger swagger down to a tee.

I remember him once saying to me, 'Hey Alf, we need to get you in a pair of heels!'

By heels, he meant cowboy boots, and I was all for it.

I did end up buying pair of authentic cowboy boots, but having a broader foot, I could never get the bloody things on. And if I did manage to squeeze my feet into them, I couldn't get them off again.

The two of us would go hiking together all the time and, my word, Pierre could trek up a mountain like nobody's business. He'd shoot up hills like a mountain goat. Quite often, on hikes, we'd go swimming in rivers: natural swimming, where you just strip off and throw yourself into running water. It was just incredible, utterly beautiful. Connecting with the wild.

I think I saw an older version of myself in Pierre, or at least that's what I wanted to see. I certainly saw something I wanted to have, something I was grasping for. It was the excitement I was drawn to, the sense of risk, the idea of living on the edge. It was the thrill of the ride, the fast pace, of throwing yourself down a mountain on a pair of skis without thinking about it, doing over 100 miles per hour on a motorbike or speeding through the mountains in his car – or even just running up a hill or a mountain.

At the time, I had to be mindful, though. Going up to Idaho to be with Sarah and the family was more important. That time was precious because I travelled so much with work. As much as I loved hanging out with Pierre, it wasn't something I could do every day. I made sure Pierre didn't monopolise my time. Once he got a hold, he didn't like to let go.

I've talked before about the time – the very memorable occasion – when the craziness with Pierre went to another level. It's definitely worth a mention for those who don't know the story. I'd just returned from the UK and visited Idaho with Sarah's dad, fly fishing. My brother-in-law and one of his friends were there too. It's something I'd never tried but really wanted to. How hard could it be? Answer? Too bloody hard.

So, there I was with a rod and reel, and I had the flies, and I was trying . . . but I just couldn't cast properly. I couldn't do it. Sometimes the hook would catch the back of my head, and I'd scratch myself and swear, and then the line would get tangled up and I'd swear again. There was a lot of swearing. In the end, I got so frustrated with the whole process, standing there up to my knees in cold running water, trying to catch a bloody fish that I was going to chuck back again anyway. It was like, what is the point of this? In the end, I put the rod down and called over to my fishing buddies.

'You know what, I'm done!' And off I went.

At first, I wasn't quite sure where I was stropping off to, but then I found myself en route to Pierre's house, which was probably a three-mile hike from where I'd been fishing – or not fishing.

I called Pierre. 'I'm on my way to your place, and you'd better have a beer ready for me when I get there.'

'You got it,' he said, without any questions.

When I walked into his house, Pierre looked at me, nodding slowly.

'You look stressed, Alf,' he said.

'I am, and I'm tired, man. I've just flown back to the States and I'm away on a guys' weekend at the cabin. I should be with Sarah and the kids at home, but here I am, fly fishing, or trying to. I can't do it; it's useless and I've had enough.'

'OK, well why don't you take a seat in the truck?' Pierre said.

'Where are we going?'

'Let's just take the dogs out for a walk,' he said, but there was something in his eyes that told me there was more.

I climbed in the truck and Pierre followed me out, carrying an old, broken TV, which he threw in the back. I didn't ask what it was for; maybe he was planning on dumping it somewhere.

His dogs, a border collie called Mudgie and a lovely Jack Russell called Josie, jumped into the back of the truck with the broken telly while Pierre bounded in the driver's seat, and then drove us along a mountain trail and up into the hills. I was quiet on the way, still in a bad mood about being the worst fisherman in Idaho. Eventually, we stopped in a small clearing where we climbed out, and walked the dogs up a hill and back down again. Once the dogs were safely back in the truck, I watched as Pierre pulled the TV from the back.

'Stay here,' he said, all very mysterious.

Surely he's not dumping it here, I thought.

Pierre placed the TV on a mound of dirt, then climbed back in the truck and started backing away from the television.

'What are you doing, man?'

'Sit there,' he said. 'You'll see.'

He pulled over again and went to the back of the truck again. I swivelled around in my seat to see him opening up a case, and when he came back, he handed me a .357 Magnum.

'Here's your gun, here's your box of cartridges. Now shoot that TV!'

'What? Are you kidding?' I'd never shot a handgun in my life.

'Yep! Get rid of all that frustration,' he said. 'Shoot the hell out of it!'

Pierre got out his Smith & Wesson revolver while I stood there with my .357 Magnum, which is a pretty hefty cannon with a revolving barrel. It all felt quite surreal and unnatural, and if I was to think of ways of coping with anger and frustration, I'm sure this wasn't the healthiest. Still, I loaded the gun, shoved some rolled-up tissue in my ears, and then pointed it at the TV. Boom! I fired, shooting it right through the screen. The kickback was strong; I wasn't expecting that kind of force. The TV exploded.

'That was incredible and awful at the same time.'

Soon enough, I was just firing away, arm jolting, watching the exploding TV in the distance.

I continued shooting away until, at one point, a mountain biker came careering down a nearby trail out of nowhere, straight into the line of fire. Despite the fact he could see us, he didn't seem in the slightest bit fazed, nor did he slow down. Of course, we saw him too, and Pierre signalled for us to lower our guns. As I pointed mine at the ground, there was a thunderous bang.

I leapt back, realising I'd accidentally shot a bullet right between my feet into the ground. I couldn't believe my eyes. I seriously could have just as easily shot my foot off.

Meanwhile, the biker happily rode straight across the plateau, through the firing line, without batting an eyelid.

'Hey guys, how you doing?' he called out like it was just routine to come across two grown men firing handguns at an old TV in the middle of nowhere. 'Have a good day.'

The two of us laughed about that for a moment, and then once he was gone, we carried on shooting.

On another occasion, Pierre took me down another trail where we shot cans off stones. It was fun for me, I guess, playing cowboys. There was no one close by, no one to harm, but Pierre sometimes took things that one step too far. One day, he handed me a gun and a bottle of Kentucky bourbon, which didn't seem like the best idea but I went along with it anyway, mainly because there was no one around as far as the eye could see. All of a sudden, it was like I was looking down on myself, shooting cans off an old stone wall while drinking whiskey.

Despite the adrenaline rush it gave me, I thought, *This can't go on for too much longer*. I lowered my gun; put it down.

'Pierre, I can't do this anymore,' I said.

'OK, Alf,' he said, cool as anything.

I'll admit there was a certain amount of excitement in shooting a gun, but in the end, I was more concerned about hitting a target than I was about the power of holding a deadly weapon, especially when fuelled by bourbon. This was the limit for me.

I have one other special memory of Pierre, from the day he let me take his treasured souped-up BMW M5 for a drive. I got it up to 155 mph – the fastest it had ever gone, he said. On the way back, driving through the mountain valley, he played 'No Expectations', by The Stones, from their 1968 album, *Beggars Banquet*.

It's an amazing song with beautiful lyrics and, when I hear it now, I recall that day vividly. It came towards the end of my time with Pierre. After that, his life took a different turn. He hit hard times.

Even though he was a social worker by profession, some-one who helped others, it made me sad to see that he was unable to help himself. He struggled with addictions and with his mental health, which eventually led to a decline in his physical health.

Sadly, Pierre is no longer with us. He'd lived on the edge, ridden bikes at crazy, crazy speeds, and thrown himself off mountains on skis, but in the end, it was cancer that got him. Pierre got prostate cancer in 2016, which destroyed him men-tally as well as physically because it took away so much. The disease and the treatment took away the man he was. He was never really himself again.

I spoke to him a couple of weeks before he died. I was

about to perform with Pete Townshend, and Pierre was a big fan of Pete and The Who – he loved their rock 'n' roll wildness. We often played their classic, 'Baba O'Riley' when we hung out together. For him, the music of bands like The Who and The Stones reflected his life; they were his life's soundtrack. He was thrilled with the idea that I was performing with the legendary Pete Townshend. During the call, I made a promise to come back and see him in February.

'I hope I'm still around by then, Alf,' he said.

He died not long after our conversation.

It's ironic and perhaps fateful that I should have met someone like Pierre, from whom I learned so much about survival, but who, when life dealt him a terrible hand, did not survive.

Still, I think that the wildness he had, the glint of danger in his eyes and the risks he took in his life drew me to him. I'll always imagine him rocking away in those Idaho hills. Inside, my logical side told me, *Don't go too far, Alfie. Don't push yourself so close to the edge.* But there's another part of me that compels me to drive myself to the limit, push myself hard, and sometimes to take chances, even ones that might be dangerous.

Back then, I was still trying to get to know myself. I suppose I still am. I'm still trying to see how far I can push myself before I burn out. If I'm honest, it's been my objective in all aspects of my life. I push myself hard as a singer. I always take it far as I possibly can. As a performer, at every show, I push to the absolute limit, emotionally and physically. I do it to create excitement and joy for others. It's that sense of achievement I always strive for. Whether it's riding a motorbike through the mountains, swimming under ice, falling off a bridge, dangling hundreds of feet in the air or giving the best performance I can give. It's all a challenge to see how far I can go and feel like I've achieved something.

In the end, it's about feeling good about myself. I don't know why I've always had this need to prove to myself that I'm good enough. I wish I did. What I do know is that I'm prone to insecurity; it's always there in my head. Sometimes I even find it hard to have affection for myself. To love myself.

A few years after Pierre died, when my own life met obstacles, I had to cope with some of those same pitfalls: the break-up of a marriage and the temptation to mask the pain with alcohol as he had. To make myself 'Comfortably Numb', as the Pink Floyd song says. Another of Pierre's favourites.

I often thought about him while I was going through my darker moments, and although I went through hell at the time, I knew eventually that I'd have to pick myself up and get back on track. If I didn't, I'd likely go down the same road as Pierre. So, I guess, in many ways, I was still learning from him, even after he'd gone.

● ● ●

My family, the cabin, Pierre, our beautiful house in the canyon. Sometimes, I felt like I didn't deserve any of it. Like many kids, I was often told in childhood, 'You don't deserve this or that,' and I guess the notion stayed with me. That somehow, I wasn't deserving of all the wonderful things I'd achieved.

Still, our time in Salt Lake will stay with me forever. Sarah created such a great environment and a lovely home for all of us. It was one of those places where you could look out of any window and see something spectacular, and that helped me discover the power and the serenity of connecting with the natural world.

The previous owner had had an office that I'd converted into a music room. One morning, I was sitting there playing my guitar when two stags sauntered into view through my window. They were huge animals; a beautiful red colour, with proud antlers, standing there, contentedly demolishing the rose garden. Amazing!

We also had a raccoon who regularly came to our bedroom door, looking for food, which I'd put out on the bird table for him. Initially, when he saw me through the window, he scarpered and I didn't see him till the following day. After seeing me in the room a few times, he started to get a bit more confident and hang around. The more he saw me, the more comfortable and at ease he seemed with me. One night, as he approached the floor-to-ceiling window, I sat down on the floor, cross-legged, and put the palm of my hand against the glass. Slowly, the raccoon approached, sniffing at my hand through the window pane. I leaned forward until our faces were only separated by glass; I could see the colour of his eyes and the matted fur on his body – it was a lovely moment. The following day, he came back with his family – his missus and the babies – it was almost as though he wanted me to meet them, so brought them for a visit.

Moments like that, being up close to wild animals and in nature, gave me so much spirit and strength. It wasn't just the sights, but also the sounds: of the trees, the rivers and the wildlife. I love the idea that, as a musician making music, you're tapping into that, adding to the landscape of nature and what is natural. Throwing myself into a freezing lake, hiking up a mountain, or getting up close to a wild animal gives me the same joy as singing a powerful song, or performing at London's Royal Albert Hall. Perhaps that's why there are so many songs about rivers, mountains and skies.

Despite the idyllic home we'd created, Sarah and I were both facing challenges within our marriage. With me leaving and going on the road so often, it was putting an increasing pressure on Sarah. It was also tough for me sometimes, coming home and readjusting to family life. It might sound odd, but now and then I felt almost like I was a guest in my own house, a visitor trying his best to fit in with everyone else's routine.

When you're away on tour, you're with a group of people connected by the music; you're creating something and performing together every night. You're experiencing something quite beautiful and unique. When you're on stage in front of an audience, you're all on the same high during the show and then, afterwards, you celebrate with one another. The shared experience often builds a strong unit of friends – another family if you like – but that can be hard for the people outside that group.

I think Sarah sometimes felt it was hard to fit into that world whenever she visited me on tour. I did my best to include her and bring her in, but I don't think she felt like she belonged.

It was the same when I came back to the family after a long stint away. Sarah always did her best to make me feel like I was home, I know she did, but I sometimes felt lost. There were times, I think, when we both felt like aliens in one another's worlds. Fortunately, in those days, we were strong enough to overcome the stresses and move on.

I didn't know it then, but I'd end up living back in Salt Lake once more a few years down the line. It wouldn't be the same, though. This time it wouldn't be a happy situation for anyone, and I'd be on my own.

CHAPTER 4

A PIECE OF ENGLAND

I was increasingly busy and travelling a lot, drawn back to the UK much of the time for some significant work-related events. One of the biggest around that time was the Queen's Diamond Jubilee concert in June 2012. It was amazing, just fabulous. The concert was held outside Buckingham Palace on 4 June of that year, organised by Gary Barlow as part of the Jubilee celebrations over the bank holiday.

For the main show, we performed on a specially built stage around the Queen Victoria Memorial, but that night, I was performing 'Somewhere' from *West Side Story* with American soprano Renée Fleming on the royal balcony, which I was especially thrilled about. Renée is a fantastic singer, a big star, warm-hearted and very down-to-earth.

I remember there being a lot going on in the run-up to our performance. There were all sorts of TV company people running about, overseeing the live broadcast. We all had one shot to get this right, and it was a big deal. There were so many technical issues to consider, too. For instance, as the orchestra were down on the stage, we had to hear them relayed through a speaker – so timing was everything. With people milling around us left, right and centre, I was trying to stay as calm as possible while Renée was busy wondering how she was going to fit on the balcony given the size of her dress.

It was such a special moment for us both, stepping onto the balcony on that beautiful, clear summer night, with the sweeping strings of an orchestra playing and projections of blossoming flowers adorning the facade of the palace. I remember thinking, look at us! We're at Buckingham Palace, on a royal balcony, looking down The Mall at a crowd that seemed to stretch for miles. With that view and our voices soaring across the crowd, it was quite spectacular. And a real honour.

Renée and I were to be the first civilians allowed to stand on a royal balcony at Buckingham Palace. Before that night, only members of the Royal Family were allowed, so the fact that we were up there was momentous.

Earlier in the day, I'd given a solo performance of 'O Sole Mio' going into Elvis Presley's 'It's Now or Never' as part of the main concert. I was wearing black jeans, boots, a cowboy shirt and an oversized belt buckle. This was around the time when I was really starting to blur the line between classical songs and other genres in the music I was singing, and I suppose the way I looked reflected that. As these two songs are basically the same melody, we did a mash-up of the two versions. I did 'O Sole Mio' with its classic Neapolitan arrangement, then Gary Barlow's band, who were the house band that night, kicked into a rocking version of 'It's Now or Never'. At that point, I started to swing my hips and go a bit crazy. I'm not sure it was what people were expecting of me, and, to be honest, I'd been a bit nervous about doing it! Luckily, it was one of those wonderful events where no one was there to criticise. It was designed simply to be enjoyed and to celebrate the Queen. The audience certainly seemed to love my Elvis switch anyway; as I started to sing the opening line of 'It's Now or Never', huge groups of them up got up on their feet and began dancing.

The line-up for the show was outrageous! Elton John – who kindly invited me to tea at The Lanesborough at Hyde Park Corner, along with Annie Lennox before the show – performed 'Your Song', 'Crocodile Rock' and 'I'm Still Standing'. Also on the bill were Robbie Williams, Sir Paul McCartney, Stevie Wonder, and the amazing Grace Jones, who performed 'Slave to the Rhythm' while hula-hooping through the entire number in a mad but glorious red head-dress. Grace was absolutely lovely, a beautiful woman who gave the impression of being a real mother figure. I spent quite a bit of time chatting with Grace about her family and her kids; she was so vibrant and energetic, but I found her very easy to talk to.

I wish I was always that smooth when meeting other celebs, but alas, that wasn't the case. That day, Cheryl Cole, as she was then known, was in the dressing room next to mine. I'd had a crush on her since the early days of Girls Aloud, so when she popped in to say hello, I got quite flustered and fell off my chair. It wasn't one of my coolest moments, but Cheryl did a fine job of pretending not to notice, which was nice of her.

Comedian Lee Mack, who was also a guest on the show – and who I didn't fall off a chair for – was writing his autobiography at the time, and at one point during the post-show-gathering to meet Her Majesty, he approached me to ask a favour.

'Alfie, would you mind taking a picture of me when I shake hands with the Queen?'

'Man, I can't do that! How can I take a picture without her seeing me do it? It feels really awkward.'

'Alfie mate, don't mess this up,' he said, handing me a professional camera with a huge lens – not exactly subtle. 'There's the camera, make sure you get the shot.'

Feeling incredibly self-conscious as Lee stepped forward to meet Her Majesty, I just pointed the camera in the general direction of the scene without really looking and snapped. What came out was a picture of the side of Lee's head with Lenny Henry over his shoulder, a tiny bit of Her Majesty's hair and cheek, and, smack bang in the middle of the shot, Kylie Minogue. To be fair, it was a decent picture of Kylie, and hilariously, it found its way into Lee's book anyway, along with the story behind it. The moral of this story is, don't ask me to take your picture.

Unfortunately, the glamour of the event was cut short later that evening. On arrival at the VIP after-party, I was stopped by security, which, as you can imagine, was fairly tight that night.

'You need to have your passport, sir,' I was told.

'What?'

'Your passport. Everyone has to have their passport for ID purposes, or there's no entry.'

I didn't have it with me, so pleaded my case.

'But I've just been singing on that balcony over there. I was singing for Her Majesty.'

'I'm sorry, but if you don't have it, we can't allow you in.'

'But . . .'

They stood there, surly-faced, not having any of it. In the end, I sadly missed the party, as did Stevie Wonder, who didn't have his passport either.

Still, that was to be just one of many performances I'd give in front of the Royal Family. Four years later, in June 2016, I was invited back to perform at Her Majesty's 90th Birthday Concert, held in the grounds of Windsor Castle. The show boasted an impressive collection of stars, including Kylie Minogue, Shirley Bassey, Andrea Bocelli, James Blunt and Beverley Knight, plus there was a generous sprinkling of British acting talent in attendance. This was a night steeped in grandeur, with every division of the armed forces and performers from all across the Commonwealth putting on an outstanding show to celebrate the life of Her Majesty. It was actually quite humbling to be part of it all.

There were so many stars on the bill that night, all performing epic numbers, while actors like Damian Lewis, Imelda Staunton and Helen Mirren narrated historic moments from the Queen's life in front of magnificent stage scenes. I was to be introduced by Dame Helen Mirren but the backdrop to my performance of a wartime classic wasn't quite what I expected.

The stage had been erected on the edge of the horse parade grounds – a huge expanse of space. When Gary Barlow opened the show with a song from his musical *Finding Neverland*, everyone knew it was going to be a night to remember. During his song, a troupe of royal guards marched in time, and a fleet of Union Jack-adorned Jaguar sports cars swept around the arena. In the middle of the song, a firework display went off along the perimeter, and the number ended with the Jags speeding around again, now flying Union Jacks behind them. Wow!

A little later in the evening, Kylie Minogue sang, 'I Believe in You', while a gorgeous display of parading horses augmented her performance, along with this wonderful horse whisperer. Kylie, in all white, shimmered under the most beautiful lighting – it was spectacular. Go, Kylie!

Before my performance that night, I'd met the Queen, who asked, 'What have you got to sing for us this evening, Alfie?'

'Well, it's one of your favourite songs, ma'am,' I proudly told her. "A Nightingale Sang in Berkeley Square."

'Oh, that's not my favourite,' she said with a smile. 'How predictable.'

Thankfully, the two of us had met before, and so I knew she was just having a little joke with me. We fist-bumped and she walked on (not really!)

When the time came, I was ready to put everything into that performance for Her Majesty. I had Dame Helen watching from the wings and an audience of millions – this had to be *magnificent*. However, after Gary Barlow's flags and sports cars and Kylie's beautiful horses, what unfolded in the arena during my song was basically an episode of *Dad's Army*. Suddenly, as I opened my mouth to sing, there were sirens, wounded bodies stretchered across the arena and nurses loading them into ambulances, soldiers changing tyres on trucks, people in 1940s clothes dashing around, and a mobile tea truck. It was like a riot breaking out in front of me. I knew it was supposed to simulate an air raid, but it wasn't easy to keep focused. There I was, belting out this gorgeous, heart-rending song, while ambulance lights flashed and people were being carted across my eye-line on stretchers, covered in bandages. Who could have heard a bloody nightingale sing over all that?

• • •

Alongside the grand public performances I was invited to give by the Royal Family, I was lucky enough to be invited to Windsor Castle on a personal level, several times. It all came about after being a musical guest on Michael Parkinson's TV show in 2007. While there, I met Michael's assistant, Autumn Kelly, who, around the time, got engaged to Peter Phillips, the son of Princess Anne and Captain Mark Phillips. I'd done a few bits and pieces with Michael around that time – I sang at his pub out in the country and performed some classical arias at the Music of Morse concert, celebrating some of the best music featured in the TV show, which Michael hosted.

After recording the TV show, Michael had invited me and Sarah to dinner at The Wolseley, and Autumn brought Peter along. Sarah and Autumn got on well, so the four of us ended up being good friends. I even sang at their wedding at Windsor Castle in 2008.

After that, Peter and Autumn would come to us for Sunday lunch, or we'd go over to their place. It became a strong friendship over the next few years.

Every year around Christmas, Peter was invited to his grandmother's home for a festive celebration and was always allowed to bring a few guests. As you can imagine, Sarah and I were thrilled when in 2018, he invited us, along with a few of his other friends, to have dinner at Windsor Castle with Her Majesty.

I was in awe as we turned up to the castle that evening. Just being inside that revered building and the honour of being invited meant so much to me. On arrival, we were greeted by a member of staff who took us to our rooms for the night, where we dressed for dinner, and then we went down to join Her Majesty for festive drinks in her private quarters.

I'm not sure what I'd been expecting the Queen's sitting room to look like, but this was a beautiful space: homely and cosy with family pictures, souvenirs and a surprisingly old-fashioned TV. In fact, with the log fire burning away, it didn't feel like a room in a castle at all – more like going to your friend's grandmother's house.

When Her Majesty arrived, she was accompanied only by her corgis, who playfully scampered around her feet. She spent time chatting with all her guests, and I'm very happy to report that she loved my jokes – even though they were pretty bad. Don't ask me what they were now because I can't remember. Her Majesty laughed, though, I swear. In fact, my fondest memories of the Queen, having met her several times, are seeing her smile and laugh. When she laughed, she really laughed; it was no polite giggle, and she made no apologies for it.

I also loved how grounded she always was and the way she made you feel welcome in her home. She seemed to enjoy people just being themselves around her. I think after all those years of meeting people, she could see through someone trying to be something other than they were, and she clearly didn't suffer fools gladly.

On that night, I had the honour of sitting next to her at the table. As far as I know, that was all Peter's doing – he somehow made sure I was seated next to her. No pressure, mate, it's only my nan. The Queen!

We ate venison with roast potatoes and vegetables, followed by chocolate fondant, and the wine and port flowed. I chatted with her about families, homes and holidays after the first course, and then she swapped to talk to the person sat on the other side of her. That was the etiquette. Then it was back and forth until all three of us engaged in conversation.

Her timing, of course, was immaculate, and I loved every moment of being there in her company.

At one point, I looked down at the corgis, Candy and Vulcan, who were sitting at our feet, eagerly waiting for any scraps that might happen to fall.

'Can I give the dogs a little bit off my plate, ma'am?' I asked.

'No, you can't, Alfie,' she said, sharply. 'They'll never leave you alone.'

And that was the end of that.

I was invited back to Windsor the following Christmas period, only this time Peter's invited guests went without their partners – it was just the guys. I watched the horse racing with her that day, and I remember her getting quite irate when her horse didn't win. It felt like a privilege to see her in her home environment.

For that occasion, I had decided to make up a hamper for Her Majesty, with local preserves, honey and some chocolates. I also bought her a hot-water bottle, which went in the hamper as well. Looking back, it makes me smile that I would have thought to buy a hot-water bottle for the Queen. She probably had several! My thinking was, if it was my grandmother I was going to see, what would I buy her? Yes! A hot-water bottle with a fine fleece cover, of course! After I'd proudly presented the gift to her that night, it was taken up to her room before she had a chance to look at it. But a while later, I received a letter of thanks followed by a phone call from her office relaying Her Majesty's apologies for not having had the chance to thank me for the lovely hamper. She was clearly thrilled!

A couple of weeks after this second visit, I took delivery of some rather special rose trees, with roses bearing my name. A couple of years before, Philip Harkness (rose breeder and head of Harkness Roses) had asked if he could grow a rose for me, so I went along to his nursery to see how they all germinated and flourished. While there, I was invited to choose the rose to be named after me. Philip showed me quite a few different varieties, but when I spotted a gorgeous, bursting, yellow bloom standing tall, I knew it had to be that one.

It took a couple of years to breed and grow my rose – probably some glue and a bit of sticky-back plastic as well – but just as it was due to be debuted at the 2020 Chelsea Flower Show, Covid hit, and the show was cancelled, going online only. Typical! Still, here they were, finally being delivered, so of course, I had to send one to Her Majesty.

A few weeks after sending the rose, I received a handwritten letter from Windsor Castle.

Dear Alfie,

What a delightful present has appeared here! Thank you so much for the rose named after you – I shall have it placed among my collection of roses here and hope to see it flower in the summer. The Chelsea Flower Show is a very good place to have a plant named – you are very fortunate and I hope it has a very good future.

How nice to think of roses instead of viruses!!
Yours sincerely,
Elizabeth R

I'll never forget my conversation with Her Majesty that night over dinner at Windsor Castle. At one point, I told her, 'You know, ma'am, this has been an incredible week for me. At the start of this week, I bought myself a house in the Cotswolds, and here I am at the end of the week, sitting in your beautiful home, having dinner with you.'

'That's lovely, Alfie,' she said. 'But the thing you should relish about this week the most is buying your house.'

'Why would you say that, ma'am,' I asked.

'Well, isn't it nice to know that you own a piece of England?'

CHAPTER 5

BRING THEM HOME

After my performance at the Diamond Jubilee, tickets for my upcoming UK tour sold really well. So much so that we had to add extra dates. It meant that as well as playing London, Manchester, Glasgow and other big cities, we added shows in Blackpool, Cardiff and Nottingham. Of course, this now meant being away for the best part of two months, which was tough on both me and Sarah.

It was great then, once the tour was over, to get involved with some big performances stateside. In particular, the Memorial Day concerts in Washington. Those are events I'm so proud to have been a part of, especially as a British artist. They're similar to the Festival of Remembrance that we have in the UK, but on a US platform. They're huge occasions, held on Memorial Day weekend, focused on remembering and honouring those who have died while serving their country in the military. The concert is broadcast and seen by military personnel in 175 countries and on US ships based all over the world. It's a big deal!

We'd been living in Salt Lake City for four years when I was first asked to do it in 2013. I realised it was quite the event to be a part of, so I started to educate myself a little bit more so I could take on board the history and significance of the occasion.

In Washington, on the day of the service itself, Sarah and I got up very early and walked around the city, through the parks and around some of the important historical landmarks: the Washington Monument, the Lincoln Memorial, and also the World War II and Vietnam Veterans memorials. I felt like I needed to see it all, to reflect on why I was there. The sights were humbling and inspiring.

Along the way, I ran into a few veterans and we spoke. I found the emotion behind their patriotism very moving. They seemed so dedicated.

'What are you doing here in Washington?' One of them asked, a middle-aged guy with a rugged face.

'Well, I'm actually here to sing at the Memorial Day service,' I said. 'I'm singing "Bring Him Home" from *Les Misérables*.'

'Well, that sounds pretty cool,' he said.

I knew there was a poignancy in performing that particular song, as a number of soldiers attending the event had just returned from Iraq. In fact, one of the mottos of the Prisoner of War/Missing in Action movement is 'bring them home.'

'I'm a bit nervous, to be honest,' I told him. 'I've never really performed at an event like this, certainly not for an audience as big as this one will be.'

He grinned, and held out something that looked like a coin, a badge from his regiment. I opened my palm, and he pressed it into my hand.

'Don't be nervous,' he said. 'Just stand there on that stage, hold this tight in your hand and think about all the POWs, the veterans, and the servicemen and women you're singing for. You'll know why you're here.'

'OK, I will.' I was slightly taken aback.

'Don't you forget now,' he said, his voice cracking with emotion.

'I won't forget, I promise.'

When it came to the performance on the West Lawn of the US Capitol Building, I was full of nervous energy. Walking out onto the stage at dusk, enveloped by the projections of stars and stripes all around me, I was facing not only an audience of half a million people plus senators, generals, dignitaries, veterans and their families, but also the famous Capitol Building itself.

As I headed for the microphone, I recalled what my veteran friend had suggested and did exactly that. I looked out over the sea of people before me, squeezed the coin tight in my palm and thought about the many who'd given their lives and service, past and present. As I stepped forward to sing, a calm came over me. Any nerves I had were swept away by the pride I felt. It was no longer about me; it was now about what

I was there to represent. In many ways, I do consider myself to be a patriotic guy, and although this wasn't my country of birth, I felt a connection with the US servicemen and service women and their families. I felt like I was singing for their armed forces and ours too.

Through doing these Memorial Day concerts – as I'm writing this, I've now done four of them – I've met more Hollywood actors and stars than you can shake a stick at. But one meeting really sticks in my mind. It was the Memorial Day event in 2016 and I was performing Bob Dylan's 'Forever Young'. It's a fantastic song and somehow perfect for the occasion. When I arrived for my rehearsals and soundcheck, one of the show's organisers greeted me as I got out of the car.

'You're up next for on-stage rehearsal, Alfie,' he said. 'The preceding artists are still doing their thing at the moment, but you can just stand at the side of the stage and hang out if you want.'

As I got close to the stage, I heard music that sounded familiar. It was then that I realised the 'preceding artists' he'd spoken of were none other than The Beach Boys. My childhood musical heroes! I couldn't believe it. To be honest, I couldn't believe I was even in the presence of these guys, let alone watching them perform from the side of the stage. And what amazed me further was singer Mike Love striding across the stage towards me after they'd finished.

'Hey! Jean Valjean, how's it going?' he joked.

As I said hello, inside I was screaming, *Wow! Mike Love*

from The Beach Boys knows who I am! (Well, he knew who Jean Valjean was, at least.)

They performed a medley of their hits that day: 'Good Vibrations', 'California Girls', 'Sloop John B', 'Wouldn't It Be Nice?' and 'Surfin' U.S.A.' All those songs I'd listened to while tearing up and down Fleetwood Beach when I was a kid. They were, of course, absolutely superb.

When I met Mike Love and Bruce Johnston again after the show, I was amazed to discover they were actually fans of what I did, and they even praised some of my past work.

'But you're ... The Beach Boys', I said, somewhat starstruck.

If someone had told twelve-year-old Alfie that he'd one day be performing on the same stage as The Beach Boys in Washington DC, I would never have believed it. At the time, I thought I'd played it pretty cool, but thinking back, I was probably gushing like crazy.

●   ●   ●

There were so many noteworthy figures and dignitaries who attended the Memorial Day services but, to me, one of the most important figureheads there to acknowledge the veterans was General Colin Powell.

Colin was the first African American Secretary of State, serving under George W. Bush from 2001–2005, and a Vietnam vet. I met him at the first of the Memorial Day concerts I played, and we really hit it off. He was one of those people who I felt like I'd known for years, just five minutes after meeting and talking with him. There was an instant connection. Colin was raised in the South Bronx, the son of Jamaican immigrants, and had risen through the ranks of the US military. Among countless other things, he oversaw Operation Desert Storm in 1991 as Chairman of the Joint Chiefs of Staff, and the challenges faced by the US government after the 2001 terrorist attacks on the Twin Towers and the Pentagon. For a guy who'd achieved so much and held such standing and importance in America and the world, he was extremely down-to-earth. Not full of his own importance or power, just a regular family man.

It might surprise you to hear that Colin was a big fan of musical theatre. He'd watched the 25th Anniversary of *Les Mis* (which I had performed in, but more on that later) and had also done some research on the guests who were performing at the Memorial that year – something he always did.

During that first meeting, I just remember him laughing and joking with me, enthusing about *Les Mis*, and even, at one point, singing. I remember thinking, this guy is great. So warm and likeable. Out of that, a strong friendship grew. He came to see me in *Les Mis* and in *Finding Neverland* on Broadway. Whenever we saw one another, it always felt like old friends reunited; he just had that way about him.

Over time, while doing these events, many of the servicemen gave me patches, pins and badges commemorating their particular regiment or battalions. This passing on of mementoes has a long history in the armed forces. Sometimes, the servicemen I met at the festival would walk up and shake hands with me, surreptitiously palming a coin or a badge into my hand. I learned that these coins are called challenge coins, and each one is uniquely designed to represent a particular organisation, in this case, a regiment or a battalion. Receiving one signifies comradeship or unity and proves that you're a member, or honorary member, of a certain group. The passing of a challenge coin from one person to another is almost like a secret handshake. It's a ritual that's almost always performed in the presence of others but goes unseen.

Each time I performed at the Memorial Day concert, I came away with several challenge coins, which I kept and collected.

The last time I sang at the Memorial Day concert was an emotional and sad one for me, as my dear friend Colin Powell had recently passed away. I'd been so terribly sad when I heard of his passing and so I was committed to making my final performance at the Memorial Day concert the best one I'd done yet.

On the day of the Memorial concert in May 2022, actor and host Joe Mantegna made a poignant speech in memory of General Powell before I sang 'The Impossible Dream' for Colin. As I performed, I remember looking at his family, who I'd met several times and who were all sitting at the front of the audience. I felt very honoured to have been asked to pay tribute to Colin. He was an amazing guy and a good friend. I miss him terribly.

Performing at Memorial Day services has always been a big moment for me; it means the world to be involved. Like the UK Festival of Remembrance, performing in these shows gives me an opportunity to pay my respects to veterans and fallen heroes – men and women, living and passed, old and young. I have such respect for them, especially coming from a family who have served in the armed forces. My great-grandfather was in the Royal Navy, my grandfather was Merchant Navy, I had an uncle in the Black Watch infantry batallion, my brother was in the Royal Air Force, and I have nephews that have been in the forces. I'm proud of them all, particularly the achievements of my brother in the Air Force. In fact, as a kid, I wanted to join the forces myself. We had one family friend who was in the Scots Guards, and I remember longing to wear the red jacket and the Busby hat. Imagine that!

Clearly, there was a whole different path mapped out for me.

CHAPTER 6

PLAYING MY ROLE

I've always found it helpful to look for parallels between myself and the characters I take on. I'd even tried to do it with Jean Valjean from *Les Mis*; it had been a while since I'd stolen any bread or the bishop's silver, but still ... Valjean's character was all about improving himself and striving to become a better person, a better man, despite the shame of his past. I think that's something I can relate to, especially now.

In the story, Valjean has been branded – literally branded with the mark of a hot iron. No matter how he tried, no matter what he did, that mark was something he could never run away from. When I first played the role in the West End in the summer of 2010, I started off the show dressed as a convict before doing a fast costume and wig change into Jean Valjean the mayor. On my very first night, full of nerves, I forgot to change my socks during the quick change. So, I rushed back on stage dressed in all the mayoral finery but still with Valjean's convict socks on my feet. Weirdly, it was this simple act of forgetfulness that helped me stay connected to the character I was playing throughout the whole show. Whatever was happening in the story, I'd look down at my convict socks and think, *I'm still the criminal that started the show, no matter what happens in the story, I'm still that guy.* It kept me aware of who Jean Valjean was and where he'd come from. After that first night, I left the convict socks on for every single performance I did.

Another important intention for me, with any project I take on, however diverse from the last, is to demonstrate that music is music, whatever the genre. It means different things to different people who will react to it and enjoy it in many different ways.

People can sometimes be intimidated by classical music, feeling that it's too high-brow for their tastes. The truth is, it's there for everyone to enjoy – it's just music at the end of the day. That notion of classical music being exclusive has been around for many years, and it's easy to see why. When you talk about classical music, it puts a picture in your mind. It's a picture of grandeur, of red velvet curtains, chandeliers, tuxedos, elaborate frocks and costumes. The word rock says rough, hard, raw and jagged. It's something from the ground, of the earth.

The history and tradition of classical musicians wearing formal black suits and bow ties is an odd and interesting one.

It started centuries ago when they essentially performed as servants in royal houses. As time went on, orchestras were expected to wear the same as the other servants of the household, and from the late nineteenth century onwards, that meant the black-tie tuxedo, or generally a black dress or suit for women. So, whether it was a ball or high-end function, or whether the gentry had just arrived home in their hunting gear, covered in mud, the musicians would be dressed in tail suits, just like the butlers and the footman.

In the past, it's been said that I've rejected conventional classical singing, but that was never the case; I never wanted to be revolutionary or shun opera. I just wanted everything I sang to unite people and cultures with music, and there were other songs, other genres of music, that could do that. Interpreting and telling a story through a rock song felt just as powerful to me as performing an aria or classical song. Structurally they may be very different in approach and delivery, but sometimes the melodies and emotions can be quite similar – especially when you listen to some of the new compositions in opera. As far as I'm concerned, one isn't better than the other.

Quadrophenia was one of the most exciting projects to come my way, and I was ready for it. In case you don't know, it's a rock opera written by Pete Townshend of The Who, first released in 1973 as an album. In 1979, it was turned it a movie starring Phil Daniels, Leslie Ash, Ray Winstone and Sting.

By late 2014, when the idea of the project came up, I'd been experimenting with different genres of music for some time, developing a solo career outside of opera and musical theatre, and pushing myself into uncharted waters. I loved blurring the lines; of taking on a song or a character that would really challenge me.

It started with a phone call from Mark Wilkinson, president of the classical record label Deutsche Grammophon in Berlin at that time. Mark and I had worked together before – in fact, he was the guy who'd given me my record deal after I'd performed the 25th Anniversary of *Les Mis*.

'A project has come up that I want to put you forward for,' he told me. 'Have you heard of The Who album, *Quadrophenia*?'

'Of course, yeah!'

'Well, we're making a new version of the album, a symphonic version, and we're looking for a singer to play the lead role of Jimmy.'

'Oh yes, please put me forward, I'd love to do it.'

Quadrophenia is set in the mid-1960s and is the story, told through music, of a troubled working-class lad named Jimmy – a mod who struggles with the changes in society and fights against the rules imposed on him in daily life. OK, so it doesn't necessarily sound like the sort of character I'd usually play, but it's such an amazing opportunity, I jumped at the chance. I had to do this. Apart from this being a great project, I'd grown up listening to The Who – songs like 'Baba O'Riley', 'Won't Get Fooled Again' and 'Pinball Wizard'. I'd also heard songs like '5:15' and 'Love Reign O'er Me' without actually realising that they were from *Quadrophenia*. Even 'The Real

Me', which I'd loved as a kid, was, to me, just a classic song by The Who on a greatest hits compilation. Having only seen the 1979 movie of *Quadrophenia*, which is a non-musical adaptation, I had no idea those songs were part of a rock opera.

I also did a bit of research on the era in which the piece was set – the mid-1960s. The battles between rival gangs of mods and rockers on the beaches of Margate, Brighton, Clacton and Hastings. It was an era when teenagers and young people were fighting to be heard, trying to make their mark on society. The world was changing, and the music of the era, like the music from *Quadrophenia*, reflected that. A decade earlier, in the 1950s, much of the music was quite wholesome and clean-cut. True, you had your revolutionaries, like Little Richard and Presley, shaking up the status quo, but there were also a lot of slick-haired surfer boys and cute girls in pinafore dresses, singing songs about cars, girls and love. Nothing wrong with that, but it was all quite safe, I suppose. When artists like Jimi Hendrix, The Who, and The Rolling Stones cut through, everything changed. There was a darker edge to it all, and suddenly various tribes of young people emerged, all looking for something more than the hopelessness they saw in front of them.

The character I was to play, Jimmy, was one of those disillusioned young people searching for his tribe. He gets kicked out of his house, loses his girlfriend to his best mate, and his hero turns out to be a fraud. He ends up driving his scooter over a cliff, so as far as opera goes, rock or otherwise, it's classic tragedy, I suppose.

I guess young people connected with *Quadrophenia* at the time because so many of them – so many of us – have gone through trauma and felt hopeless at one time in their lives or another. I've certainly had those kinds of emotional crashes where I've driven my bike off a cliff. Figuratively, of course, not literally. When your bike goes over a cliff but you don't go with it, there's no alternative but to walk and keep on going.

Just as I had with Jean Valjean, I was keen to find a connection with this character, with Jimmy.

When the chance to sing *Quadrophenia* first came up, I thought it would be something the record label was putting together. One of those projects where someone decides to do a classical or symphony version of a rock album. I assumed I'd be working with a certain conductor and an orchestra and perhaps some other classical voices. I had no idea that it was to be Pete Townshend himself at the helm, or that the orchestrations had been done by his supremely talented wife, Rachel Fuller.

It was an incredible thing for me to be involved with. Given my love and appreciation for rock music, getting the chance to work with Pete was outstanding. Still, when I was asked to go along to record some demos with him, it transpired that although I'd been put up for the role, it wasn't quite yet in the bag.

I'd prepared a fair bit leading up to it. I'd listened to the original album, which Roger Daltrey sang on; I listened to the live version, and Pete's early demos of the songs, which were mostly just Pete and a guitar, and very different from Roger's interpretation. I learned it all. I took it all in. And when I headed to record the demos, I felt quietly confident.

Pete had a little studio on an old seafaring Dutch barge moored on the Thames in east London. It's a pretty little thing, and he does a lot of his work there. I turned up there early, listened to the new tracks – got them in my head and in my body – and thought, *Yeah! This is going to be good. I can sing this stuff, it's going to work.* Then Pete rocks up, quiet and reserved like he is, not saying very much. I smiled and said hi, but inside, I was a bit of a mess, completely in awe. Still, I was excited. Raring to go. Pete, I soon realised, wasn't quite as gung-ho.

'Now, I know you're up for this project, but let's treat this as an audition sort of thing, yeah?'

'Oh, right.'

I looked at him, blinking back at me, waiting to crack a smile and tell me he was joking. After several seconds of deadpan coming back at me, I realised he wasn't joking. This wasn't so much a recording session, it was a try-out.

'Of course,' I said.

I was a bit shaken. I mean, I thought I'd already bagged the gig, but Pete clearly had other ideas. He wanted to make sure I was right for it, and why wouldn't he? This was his baby, his masterpiece.

I walked into the vocal booth thinking, *It's fine Alfie, you can do this. No worries. You've got this, mate.*

The first track began, and I started to sing. Focused, solid, determined. After a few lines, I felt like I was getting into the swing of it. I relaxed, and my confidence grew. As the session went on, it grew to the point when I was just banging the songs out. Really letting go. I thought about Pierre, flying down the mountain on a pair of skis or doing 120 mph on a motorbike with The Who as his soundtrack, and I just went for it. I literally gave it everything I'd got. At the end of it, Pete sauntered into the vocal booth.

'That was OK', he said, still deadpan.

It struck me that this guy was either a hard man to please or just not particularly expressive. That said, I detected a little glint in his eyes that told me he was happy with what I'd done. More than happy if I wasn't mistaken.

Following that, we had to duet on one of the song demos. Standing side by side in the booth, things started off all very politely. I did my lines and stepped aside as he did his. By the middle of the song, however, we were shoulder barging each other off the microphone, vying for prime position, each trying to outdo the other. From that moment on, we became friends, and pretty soon we were good friends.

When it came to recording the album, the process was wonderful. I recorded the whole thing in four or five hours – mostly at Pete's studio in a converted stable at his house in Oxfordshire. The entire experience was everything I hoped it would be, but the live performance concert at the Royal Albert Hall in July 2015 was a real highlight. And what a line-up. It was me; Pete; Phil Daniels, who'd starred as Jimmy in the 1979 movie version; and Billy Idol, who was a great guy, very funny. In October, I performed the live show in Vienna. This time an American singer called Drew Sarich took on all the roles previously played by Pete, Billy, and Phil.

In 2017, we took the show on a tour of the US, with our original line-up. On that tour, we played two nights at the Metropolitan Opera in New York. It was probably the first time the smell of marijuana had wafted through the auditorium of that iconic hall. The thought of it makes me smile.

I suppose there's irony in the fact that after years of singing opera and classical music, the first time that I got to tread the boards at one of the greatest classical venues in the world, I was singing rock music. And what an incredibly beautiful place it is. Grand and beautiful. I loved singing there.

While we were in New York, Pete and I were invited to be the musical guests on *The Tonight Show Starring Jimmy Fallon* at the NBC studios in Rockefeller Plaza. Kris and Kylie Jenner were also guests on the show that night, and at the end of their spot, Pete and I performed 'Love Reign O'er Me' with Jimmy's house band, The Roots, plus a full orchestra.

From New York, we jumped on a private jet and flew to Chicago. There we played the Rosemont, with singer Eddie Vedder from Pearl Jam joining us on stage, Chicago being his home town. He was a sweet guy, and someone I'd always been a big fan of.

Eddie is a gentle soul, very understated, who, of course, loves music as much as I do. He's one of those performers who's very supportive of people he's sharing a stage with.

I have to say; he surprised me when we chatted backstage before the show.

'I can't begin to tell you what a huge influence you've been on my singing, Eddie', I told him. 'Now here I am, about to go on stage and sing a duet with you.'

'Wow, man, I can't believe a singer like you would say something like that to me', he said. 'That's a great compliment.'

Eddie seemed genuinely blown away that I was so inspired by him, which was a beautiful feeling.

We then, along with Billy Idol, dived into a conversation about vocal tiredness and what our various regimes and routines were for voice preservation and protecting our precious vocal cords. My voice was tired before that show; I'd been really going for it during the previous shows, and that was starting to take its toll.

In California, we played the Greek in Los Angeles. What a venue! It's such an iconic cultural landmark of the city, an amphitheatre in Griffith Park holding about 6,000 people. When the sun starts to set over LA, the light over the Greek is incredible, and when you're on stage there, you can't help feeling awe about some of the people who've performed there in the past – Aretha Franklin, Bruce Springsteen, Frank Sinatra, Elton John – the list goes on and on.

Many of Pete's old friends were there, as well as Billy's friends and family. The entire thing felt epic; there must have been over a hundred people in the LA symphony orchestra, plus a choir of maybe sixty or seventy singers. It was an outstanding show and a powerful night, although it might have gone a very different way.

I still hadn't been feeling a hundred per cent all that day. Backstage, before the show, I felt as though my voice wasn't fully there, plus I felt decidedly queasy. *Quadrophenia* is one hell of a sing, and I'd really gone for it on the shows leading up to it. I hadn't held back in Boston, sung myself out in New York, and in Chicago, my voice was really tired. By the Greek, my vocal cords felt pretty raw. Still, despite not being on top form, I knew that I could get through it. I knew I had enough in the tank to give it my best and pull a great performance out of the bag. I had to!

Half an hour before curtain up, I was introduced to a guy from a team I was working with at the time. Rather than giving me a pep talk when he strolled into my dressing room to see me – perhaps reminding me that I could do it and that the crowd were going to love me (you know, the nurturing type of thing you might expect) – this guy went the other way entirely.

'Well, Alfie, this is a hell of a platform to fall down on.' He shook his head solemnly. 'I mean, if you're going to be ill, this is probably not the best place to do it!'

'I'm sorry?'

Remember, this guy was meant to be fighting my corner, but here he was not being supportive and making me feel even more insecure than I already did.

'Well, that's a nice thing to say,' I said, feeling hurt. 'I think it's probably best if you leave now and let me prepare for the show.'

I sensed a dismissiveness in the way he'd spoken, an arrogance, and it's something I've come across more than once in the entertainment industry. There are lots of people doing all manner of important jobs, with everyone fighting their own corner. At times, it can start to feel like everyone else thinks they know best how a performer should do things. The trouble is, there are those who are more worried about how something reflects on them than they are about the well-being of their artist. When the curtain goes up, it's the performer who has to step out in front of an audience and deliver. They stand or fall on what they do. Of course, honesty is always a good thing, but I've always thought the people around you, working with you, should be there to support you rather than tear you down.

This was the final show of the tour, and the last thing I wanted to do was to let Pete down with a sub-standard performance – not to mention letting the audience down, or myself. The whole encounter shook me up, but as I walked out on stage, I thought, *That's it, I'm going to knock it out of the park.* Ultimately, the show at the Greek was, I think, one of our best. Maybe I was aware that not feeling my best meant that I really had to push it and go the extra mile. Whatever the reason behind it, we ended up blowing the roof off the place.

When the beautiful sweeping overture, 'I Am the Sea' began, with conductor Robert Ziegler leading the huge orchestra beneath the giant tricolour mod target, it felt magical. Then suddenly, I was bounding onto the stage, belting out the first line of 'The Real Me'.

It's funny, despite how I'd felt before the show, I was on top of the world performing that night. It felt like the culmination of all the hard work and love that had gone into the project over several years, and a special evening of music that I think will be cherished by everyone who came.

In the movie *A Star Is Born* with Lady Gaga and Bradley Cooper, the song 'Shallow' is first performed at the Greek. In a backstage scene, the camera pans across the little black tiles, signed by many of the artists who've played there. If you slow the movie down, you can see Billy Idol's and my signatures on the screen. I think that's quite cool. It's a special stage and a special venue.

A couple of days after that show, a woman recognised me on Sunset Boulevard. She came over, looking very excited to see me.

'That was such an incredible show at the Greek, amazing,' she said, beaming.

'That's really kind of you to say; thank you very much,' I replied, but then her face fell slightly.

'It's just a pity you guys were all miming.'

'I'm sorry?'

'Yeah, I mean, it was lovely having the live orchestra and all that, but you guys, Pete and Billy and you; why did you feel you had to mime the songs rather than singing them live? It's such a shame, it really is.'

'Er . . . we didn't mime, we were singing everything live.'

The woman shook her head. 'No, you weren't. You couldn't have been doing that live.'

'I did sing it, I did!' My voice went up an octave, wondering what on earth could make her think that I'd been lip-synching over a bloody great symphony orchestra.

'No, you couldn't have.'

Even as I walked away, having explained that everything on the stage had been fully and absolutely live, I still don't think she believed me. It made me wonder whether anyone else might have thought we were miming. In the end, I told myself that our vocals must have been so impressive, she couldn't believe they weren't recorded. Job done.

CHAPTER 7

GRAFTING

Over the years, throughout my career, I've suffered from stage fright. Ultimately, it's never brought me down or stopped me from doing what I love doing, but it's something I've had to overcome.

Back in the day, when I was playing in working men's clubs and small venues, I was still learning my craft and testing the waters. As well as trying to give the best performance I had in me, I also knew I had to hold the attention of an audience. I had to entertain them and make them like me, which often felt scary. In those days, my nerves were shocking. I was running to the bathroom to throw up before going on, and the whole idea of getting up there in front of a crowd knocked me sideways. After I'd done it, after my little spot on the bill, the energy and feeling of elation I had was wonderful. I suppose that's what kept me going back for more, despite my nerves. Once I was done, I'd always tell myself, *OK, Alf! You've done a decent job. It might not have been the best, but you did it. And next time you'll be better.*

These days, I still get nervous, but I do my best to turn it into excitement right before I'm about to go on and face the music. I use all that nervous energy to build myself up rather than letting it knock me back.

When I'm playing at an important event or a show where I'm one of many performers, this really comes into play. Like the 2014 Royal Variety Performance, which was a real milestone for me; one of those times when I had to pinch myself to make sure I wasn't dreaming. In fact, as I sat there at the dressing room mirror, preparing for the performance, I had flashbacks to my days as a stagehand in Blackpool, setting up for great artists like Shirley Bassey, who was headlining that evening.

As a teenager, I'd worked at the Winter Gardens, Blackpool Opera House as a stagehand. I'd construct the set, lay down the flooring, rig the lights and speakers and set up the drum risers before a show. Back then, if someone had told me that fifteen years later, I'd be on the bill of the Royal Variety Performance alongside some of the artists I was helping set the stage for, I would have probably just laughed at them. Now here I was, about to share the bill with Dame Shirley.

There have been other times when, for me, life seems to have come full circle. Last year, I saw Gary Barlow in his one-man-show, *A Different Stage*, which reflects on Gary's life and career in his own words. During the show, he talks about his youth, playing the northern club circuit. At one point, he said something like, 'And eventually, I found myself at the Talk of the Coast in Blackpool!'

Cue a gold curtain falling, which Gary then walks through, donning a mask and cape, and sings 'The Music of the Night', from *The Phantom of the Opera*.

'What? The Talk Of the Coast!' I was gobsmacked.

At sixteen, I was playing drums in a few bands in working men's clubs and at local events. Around that time, there was a well-known annual talent competition held at a cabaret venue called Talk of the Coast, at the Viking Hotel in Blackpool. The Viking is on Blackpool seafront, about twenty minutes' walk from the pier, so, as you can imagine, fairly popular, especially during the summer months.

Back then, in the late 1980s, the Talk of the Coast was quite renowned with some big acts of the time performing there. I remember seeing The Nolans and comedian Frank Carson there, and I met Bradley Walsh in his early days. At one point, comedian Stu Francis (yes, the bloke from *Crackerjack!*) took me under his wing, co-managing me along with the venue's compere Georgie King. They got me a few gigs at celebrity golf tournaments and the like, which weren't really the right platforms for me professionally, but at least gave me good stage experience. Eventually, when I got the chance to sing for the D'Oyly Carte Opera Company, Stu convinced Georgie that they had to let me go and spread my wings.

On the nights I performed at the Talk of the Coast, Mum and Dad, and sometimes my brothers and sisters, would be there to support me. Often, Dad would drive me there, sit in and watch me do the show, and then drive me home again. My repertoire consisted of songs like 'Somewhere' and 'Tonight' from *West Side Story* and 'True Love Ways' by Buddy Holly, but I never had sheet music or the chords for many songs – I didn't know where to get hold of that sort of thing back then – so it was hard for me to build or perfect a complete show. As well as that, the player at the venue couldn't always follow the piano music that I did bring because he was more of a keyboard player than a pianist. Consequently, I'd end up singing without accompaniment, teaching myself how to sing a cappella. As it turned out, this was a good way for me to go because these unaccompanied performances were generally the ones that brought the house down.

Back then, it was the cheesiest place and a crazy environment to perform in. Being a seaside venue in a hotel, it had an old-fashioned cabaret vibe about it, more of an adult crowd than families, with everyone sat around small tables with their pints or their gin and tonics, smoking, gabbing away, and generally having a fine old time. The stage was small with a ring of lights around it, but it wasn't much higher than the floor, so as a performer, you were quite close to the audience. I'm sure it's all been done up and is a bit more glamorous these days, but back then, it was a fairly intimate experience all round.

Also, some of the acts that played there were positively surreal. I remember one unfortunate fella coming out on stage
wearing trousers, a string vest and a pair of braces, and all he did
was make faces and point at the lights. He was billed as a comic
but literally said nothing for about fifteen minutes, trying to
build laughs around this silent character who just pointed and
made faces. It was bizarre and, I have to say, pretty terrible. Of
course, there was talent about, but among that talent, there were
terrible comedians, disastrous singers and some shocking guest
dancers. Still, it was a great place for me to learn and develop my
craft, and I went back often, building my repertoire as I went. I
guess you could say it was a bit like an apprenticeship.

It made me smile to think that a star like Gary had started
his career in entertainment at the very same place I had, singing musical theatre songs. He'd been up there belting out
songs from *Phantom* while I'd sung *West Side Story*. Now here
he was, playing tribute to that legendary place where so many
performers had started, developing their acts and sharpening
their skills.

Talk of the Coast is still going strong and seems to be a
big asset to Blackpool. I'm just looking it up now; it opens at
seven o'clock tonight. Maybe I should pop down there and
give them a blast!

Playing those kinds of clubs when you're young or up-
and-coming is like a training ground. It can prepare you for
any probability while you're up there performing. The truth
is, if you can deal with those audiences, you can deal with virtually any audience.

A few months ago, I was doing a show where a guy randomly leapt onto the stage and started dancing around me like crazy. Not something I'm generally used to happening at my shows, but there it was. I tried to keep my eye on him while I was performing, but it wasn't easy. The guy even high-fived me mid-song at one point. By then, I could sense everyone around me thinking it would end in disaster and he'd probably have to be dragged off by security. In the end, I decided the best thing to do was pull him in and give him a hug. Suddenly, the pressure was lifted, and he walked off stage happy. As the guy disappeared back into the audience, somebody shouted, 'Sorry about that, Alfie!'

'Hey, that's nothing!' I called back. 'I've played the northern clubs.'

Despite the nerves of those early days, I always had determination. That's what kept me going, I think. It's as if I had this voice in my head telling me I had something to prove, not to anyone else, but more to myself. I wanted to prove to myself that I could get up there and do it. I had this deep desire in me to entertain an audience, to make people happy, and the more realised I had it in me to do that with my voice, the more I was driven to do it.

It's where I get my strong work ethic from. A code in me that's so strong it often works to the detriment of others. I'm terrible at making plans, always changing things at the last minute, or cancelling stuff because of work. The truth is, when an opportunity for a job comes up, I see it as building a future for my children, and I find that hard to say no to.

It's often very annoying for others – especially those closest to me.

The bright side of all that is those special moments all the grafting has brought me. On that night of the 2014 Royal Variety Performance, I opened the show singing the national anthem – no pressure – and followed it up by singing 'Blue Moon', half in Italian, half in English. At the end of the show, I took my bows alongside Dame Shirley and Bette Midler. It was one of those moments when I stopped and thought, *Yeah. It's going well.* I felt very proud, as I always did when it came to an event involving Her Majesty and members of the Royal Family.

You can just imagine how bowled over I felt receiving an OBE in 2019 – that felt a very long way from the Talk of the Coast, I can tell you. The Order of the British Empire award recognises achievements in public life and recipients can come from any walk of life. They're known as Queen's Honours, but a committee has the final decision on who receives one, and most people are nominated.

A few years before, I'd been surprised to discover that my management at the time was planning to nominate me for an OBE. Unbeknown to me, they'd built up a portfolio of letters and recommendations from various quarters to put me forward. I felt a little uncomfortable about the idea at the time. It wasn't that I was against the idea of the honours system, more that this wasn't the way I wanted to go about receiving one. It felt too contrived, too forced.

When I parted ways with my management, they handed

over the folder they'd been putting together. It contained various accolades and letters from notable people, talking about my achievements, my charity work and reasons they thought I'd be a worthy recipient of an honour from Her Majesty. For a couple of weeks, I didn't know what to do with it. To tell the truth, it wasn't a great time in my life; I'd been pretty low. I certainly didn't feel like the wonderful human being all these letters described. I'd separated from my management, things with Sarah had, at times, been strained – it all felt wrong. After a couple of weeks, I came to the conclusion that it wasn't something I was going to pursue anyway, so I sat down one day at our home in Salt Lake City, picked up the folder, and lit a fire with it. One by one, I burnt every one of the letters and testimonials from some amazing people. I just didn't want to receive something so significant and momentous in that way, so it all went up in smoke. I let it all go.

Then in March 2019, I was invited to perform at the annual Commonwealth Day ceremony in Westminster Abbey in front of Her Majesty the Queen, Prince Charles and Camilla – now King Charles and Queen Camilla – William and Kate, and Harry and Meghan. I performed at the altar one of the songs I'd performed at the VE celebration; an a cappella version of Snow Patrol's song 'Run'. It was a wonderful moment for me, but a strange one. Although the congregation was large, it felt like an intimate moment between the Royal Family and me. It wasn't the same as performing on a huge stage with the family in a faraway box, as I'd done several times before. I was standing on the abbey floor with Her Majesty sitting on a chair just a few feet in front of me.

During the preparations for that day, and at the ceremony itself, I got to know some of the dignitaries and people running the event. I expressed how much I'd loved performing for Her Majesty at this and other events, and how I'd be happy to offer my services whenever called upon. It couldn't have been more than a month later when I received a letter from the Foreign Office asking me to contact them as soon as possible. My first thought was, *What on earth have I done wrong?* I hadn't a clue what the Foreign Office might want with me. After contacting them, I received an email saying they were pleased to inform me that I'd been given an honour by Her Majesty the Queen – the Order of the British Empire for services to music and charity. Of course, I was happy and honoured to accept. Over the moon. I assumed it was because of the charity work I'd done for The Prince's Trust, plus other royal-supported charities I'd been involved with. Also, for events like my performances at the Diamond Jubilee and the Queen's ninetieth birthday, as well as my recent one at the Commonwealth Day ceremony. I like to think those were the things that had given me recognition, so I was very happy with how it all had come about at that time. No portfolio, no lobbying.

The ceremony itself was an incredible day. It was a bright spot in a horrible year for me. The night before, Sarah and I booked into a suite at The Savoy with the children where we had a celebration dinner and all enjoyed a bit of luxury. The following day we all got dressed up, me in my morning suit, before piling into a posh car that drove us to Buckingham Palace.

When we arrived, I was separated from the family. They went to take their seats, and I went into a holding room with the other honourees. There were people from all walks of life there that day. All there to accept a CBE, MBE, OBE, Knighthood or Damehood. There were servicemen and service women, nurses, doctors and politicians. I must admit, though, I was kind of in a world of my own; I was so excited.

When it was time to receive our medals, we were put into an order and escorted, line by line, to the ballroom. The thing I remember most, as I was at the door waiting to walk out in front of the gathered friends and families, was looking out and seeing my kids, both yawning their heads off. I love them so much! Still, it was a hugely proud moment for me, hearing my name and achievements read out before Prince Charles pinned on my medal.

I'd met him on quite a few occasions by then, but my affiliation with him went back a long way. I'd been a Prince's Trust scholar three years in a row. As a recipient of the Queen Elizabeth the Queen Mother scholarship, part of The Prince's Trust, I could afford to go to music college and to survive, financially, while doing it. When he presented me with my Fellowship of the Royal College of Music in 2013, it was a lovely moment.

'I can't tell you, Alfie, how proud I feel to be able to give this award,' he told me.

He's a lovely guy. Someone I've always been able to laugh and crack a joke with, and someone it's always an honour to sing and perform for.

At the end of the award ceremony, once we'd taken some photographs with the family, we headed to The Wolseley, one of my favourite places, for dinner. I sat there in my morning suit with my OBE on the table, with Sarah and my children, feeling very happy and proud to have been honoured by the Queen of England. It's strange writing about it now and quite sad for so many reasons.

CHAPTER 8

ME, BUT NOT ME

B ack in those early days, I couldn't wait to be famous. I wanted the things you're expected to want as an up-and-coming performer – fame, fortune, recognition. It was all seemingly there for the taking, so why shouldn't I reach out and take it?

People have often asked me what I consider the biggest breaks in my career, and I suppose the one that first comes to mind is being accepted into the D'Oyly Carte Opera Company when I was twenty. D'Oyly Carte is a society started by a theatrical agent called Richard D'Oyly Carte in the late nineteenth century to produce the operas of Gilbert and Sullivan. Some of you will know the story of the customer who heard me singing at the TVR car factory where I worked as an apprentice mechanic – I sang a lot at work! He suggested that I audition for D'Oyly Carte (I didn't have much of a clue what he was talking about) but around the same time, my singing teacher Lawrence Newnes told me that D'Oyly Carte were holding auditions in London and I should go for it. When I bought my weekly copy of *The Stage and Television Today* to check out potential jobs and immediately spotted the advert for the D'Oyly Carte auditions, it felt like fate. I was hearing and seeing that name everywhere, so what else could I do but plan a trip to London to audition?

It was a strange chain of events, really. I'd been singing for a while by then, performing with various amateur operatic companies in Fleetwood and doing my stints at the Talk of the Coast and the working men's clubs – which meant I was singing across all different genres of music: classical, musical theatre, plus pop and rock ballads.

Once I started working at the factory, though, I kind of put singing on the back burner to concentrate on my apprenticeship. Then, after a few months, I woke up one morning with this burning inside me, this voice in my head telling me that I had to be a singer, that I had to sing and to start performing again. I couldn't stop thinking about it.

A friend who was into amateur operatics suggested I try out for the Preston Musical Comedy Society, who were about to start rehearsing a production of *West Side Story*. I think I got into the chorus without them even hearing me sing, but some of the boys in the chorus weren't happy about the casting of Tony, the principal male character. That role had already gone to an older guy who was a bit of a star in amateur operatics, without any of them having a chance to audition. In the end, the musical director, Phillip Wooley, had to give in and agree to let the boys in the chorus have a go, leading us all into a room.

'OK, I'm going to play through the song "Maria", and I want you guys to sing through it together,' Phillip said. 'All at once.'

Now, there are two ways you can sing the second part of the song. You can either repeat the name Maria over and over, or there's an alternative version where you sing the name once, sitting on a top A which carries over the whole phrase. The second version was the only one I knew. I'd listened to one of my heroes singing it many times in *The Making Of* West Side Story, the documentary which was a behind-the-scenes look at Leonard Bernstein's 1984 reimagining of his musical masterpiece with opera singers José Carreras and Kiri Te Kanawa. In that version of 'Maria', José held that beautiful top note, so that's what I did. By the time I'd finished, everyone else had stopped singing, but I was so into it, I hadn't even noticed.

After that, Phillip said, 'OK, thanks, you can all go. Alfie, can you stay back, please?'

For me, the audition continued, and I sang through some more of Tony's parts just as I knew them. Just as I'd heard José sing them. At the end of it, the director had to make a difficult call to the guy they'd originally cast, telling him he no longer had the part.

Down the line, as I trained as an opera singer, I would stand on stage at the Royal Albert Hall along with Bryn Terfel,

Kiri Te Kanawa and José Carreras. At the time, it seemed unbelievable to me that I was sharing a stage with José, someone I'd listened to, loved and admired for so long.

Looking back on those early days of auditions and dreaming big, it really was all about just singing back then. Nothing else to cloud things. No fame, success, press or scrutiny. I just wanted the chance to do what I loved. That was all.

I suppose that's why I went to the D'Oyly Carte audition, not worrying about how I'd be perceived or even how I looked. To be honest, having to dash straight into a night shift at the car factory after the audition, I didn't have much choice how I looked. I was wearing a lumberjack shirt over a sweaty T-shirt, work boots, and my jeans were splattered with paint. All I cared about when I turned up at the Peacock Theatre in London was showing people what I could do as a singer. When I walked up the stairs to the first floor to sign in, everyone else there looked pristine, all dressed up to the nines in smart suits and ballgowns. But that didn't matter to me either. It didn't even matter that the only music I had was a torn, tatty sheet borrowed from Fleetwood Library, and I had to take it back at the end of the audition. It was 'You Are My Heart's Delight', that song by Franz Lehár, which my dad used to listen to all the time. What mattered was my voice, and I suppose that's the way it should be. All the other stuff I've worried about over time came with having success. How you look and how people perceive you somehow becomes more important, and it's sometimes less about the singing, which is sad really.

I can still see myself standing in that black auditorium, so dark I could hardly make out a thing. I couldn't even see the audition panel, who were sitting on a balcony somewhere in the dark, ready to judge and assess me. I handed my sad-looking music to the accompanist, Dane Preece – a lovely guy who went on to be Head of Music at Arts Ed, one of the best performing arts schools in the UK – and started to sing.

At the end of my audition, there was ... nothing. Just dead silence. I remember thinking, *OK, I must have done something wrong.* Dane looked over at me and nodded. Suddenly a voice came out of the dark.

'Thank you, Alfie. Would you be willing to make another trip down to London at some point?'

'Er, yeah. Of course I would.'

'OK, we'll be in touch. Thank you for your time.'

I walked over to Dane, who was smiling reassuringly at me from the piano.

'Can I have my music back, please? I've got to take it back to the library,' I said.

I felt pretty good as I travelled back on the train, excited about the possibilities of what might happen and sure enough, a few weeks later, I got a phone call asking me to come back down to London for another audition. I remember at the time, my main concern was asking my foreman for another day off work!

I didn't even know what kind of singer I was when I went for that call-back audition in the basement of a church in Maida Vale. There I met the musical director, John Owen Edwards.

'Are you a tenor or a baritone?' he asked me.

I didn't know the answer. I knew I loved singing and had a grasp of what I was capable of, but I really had no idea what that was called in musical terms because nobody had ever told me.

'I have no idea to be honest,' I said.

John smiled and said, 'Well, let's find out, shall we? Let's go through some scales.'

John sat at the piano and began playing scales, with me singing along. He led me higher and higher until, eventually, I hit a Top C.

'Oh, right!' John said. 'I think you're a tenor.'

'OK, that's good to know.'

After that, I sang through the songs from *West Side Story* that I'd brought along and then took the train back home.

One of the best parts of that experience was my mum and dad's reaction when I got the phone call from Ian Martin, the managing director. As I took the call on the phone in the hall of our house, I knew full well they were huddled on the other side of the living room door, listening to every word. I think they were more nervous and excited than I was.

'We'll get you an Equity card, Alfie,' Ian said. 'And we'd like to offer you a place in the chorus of the D'Oyly Carte. Do you think you'd be interested, and would you be able to hand in your notice at work?'

'Yes, I'd love to. Thank you very much; I'm very grateful.'

And I was! This was a full-time professional job as a singer.

Back in the living room, Mum and Dad were sitting down again, twiddling their thumbs nervously.

'I got it,' I said. 'They've offered me a job.'

Mum and Dad both burst out crying, bless them. It was a memorable moment. This was the break that first turned my life around. It was the hand that opened the door and set me on the journey I'd been longing to begin.

When fame happens, when a person becomes 'famous', it often feels different from what they'd expected. At least, it did for me. I always imagined that once I'd cracked into the business and got a big break, it would be plain sailing from thereon in. My voice would open up the world and carry me through, and that was all I'd have to worry about. You'll probably not be surprised to hear that wasn't the case.

That particular notion, borne, I suppose, out of youth and innocence, was ripped away after I did my first big opera in 2000, playing Rodolfo in David McVicar's production of *La Bohème* at Glyndebourne. I had such anticipation of getting my first proper review for an opera, especially knowing how hard I'd worked and how much I'd put into it. I was excited about it because I'd sung it to the best of my ability, and the audience's reaction had been so fantastic. In my mind, the review would be glowing, setting me on an amazing upward course, career-wise. When I opened one paper to the reviews page, that dream fell away fast. I can't remember exactly what it said, but it was something along the lines of, *Alfie Boe's voice is clearly a little immature for the role of Rodolfo*, and it only got worse from there. It was a shock, and I wasn't ready for it. The worst part about it was that I had to get back up on stage two days later and do it again, with that reviewer's words rattling around in my head.

The thing is, nobody teaches you how to deal with bad reviews and negative press – well, nobody taught me anyway. I just remember thinking at the time, why is this person saying those nasty things about me? I'd worked so hard that night; it was a great show, and I sang my heart out. It was a proper slap in the face, and after that I said to myself, *Buckle up, Alfie! This is going to be harder than you thought. It ain't all gonna be handed to you on a plate.*

Two things I had to learn fast were that you can't control someone else's opinion, but on the other hand, that person is only one voice in an auditorium full of people. It's just a shame when 'that voice' has such a sizeable platform for their opinion, so lots of other people get to hear it.

The unfortunate add-on when I *did* become famous was that those opinions and voices carried over from professional criticisms to commentary on my personal life. Although I'm not sure I can even pinpoint when that was. Maybe it was when I started performing at national events and appearing on TV regularly. Or maybe it was when people started to recognise me in public and ask for autographs and photos. I guess you're famous when you're a question on a TV show.

'Which English tenor used to be a car mechanic?' Or *'Name the English tenor who sings with Michael Ball?'*

I don't really have any resentment for the press, though, despite being on the receiving end of some pretty harsh reporting on occasion. I know people have a job to do and families to feed, and writing about celebrities is the job of some journalists. That's not to say it doesn't hurt when I read something negative about myself, especially when it's only half the story or, as has been the case many times, completely off the mark.

I suppose thoughts about fame and how important it is – or isn't – changed when I had my children. When kids come into the picture, it really puts life into perspective. After Grace and Alfie came along, my life wasn't just about me anymore; it was about them and what I could give them. Suddenly, my career was more about what it meant in terms of looking after my family. The fame, the recognition, and everything else was a means to an end, a way to make a decent living doing the best job I possibly could. For them.

I think that's why, these days, reading negative articles or untruths about myself and my family hits even harder, especially when all I want to do is get on with doing what I do best – entertaining. We've all seen how some people are affected by things written about them. We've seen the tragedy of someone in the public eye who has been hounded and can't cope anymore. I find it sad that we still hear those kinds of stories, of people suffering trauma or mental health problems because of public opinion and the so-called freedom of the press to write whatever they feel like writing, with little or no accountability.

It's got worse over the last decade. Back at the start of my career, I only had to worry about a newspaper gossip column or a trashy magazine weighing in with opinions on my private life. Now, with social media platforms as big as they are, everyone can have their say, and it's all out there for the world to see.

• • •

The smart thing to do is ignore it and focus on the work, but that's not always easy. It's definitely the most important thing, though: the work and the audience I'm performing for. The people who are paying money to buy my music and come and see my shows. That's what matters most.

It's why, without a doubt, my favourite thing about my job now is touring. It's what I enjoy doing the most. Being on the road, travelling from city to city and walking into a new venue, the anticipation of the show starting, walking out onto a stage, performing each night, and then meeting the fans after the show. That's a big thing for me, getting to say hello to the people who have supported me over the years. That's one of the best things fame has given me.

When I'm on one of my solo tours, I prefer travelling with the band on the tour bus. After a show, we'll get out of our stage clothes and out of whatever theatre we've been playing in, and then climb on the bus and chill out for a while. We'll listen to music, have some food, a few drinks and a laugh. It's a good feeling, climbing into the bunk and falling asleep to the motion of the bus on the road, only to wake up in a brand new town.

Sill, as much as I love the thrill of a tour, the nerves always get me. Yes, I still have that stage fright I had when I was young. Fame doesn't change that. I suppose now I deal with pre-stage jitters in the same way I dealt with jumping into a frozen lake in the Alps. Deep breathing, slowing it all down, calming myself to the point where I'm focused and ready to walk out on stage.

Once I'm on stage I become somebody else. Me, but not me. I don't want to compare myself to Freddie Mercury, but while that great man was offstage, he was Farrokh Bulsara, a shy and studious guy. But he walked on stage as Freddie Mercury, the rock star, ready to blow the roof off. It was almost like a character he was playing, and I suppose I do something similar. That brash guy who's out there giving it large and belting out songs is someone I can hide behind. He gives me licence to live out my childhood dreams of being a performer. I couldn't possibly be that guy off-stage, 24/7. Now that would be scary. Loud and scary.

One of my favourite places to perform is Japan. There's something wonderful about the culture and history of the country, and yes, I'm quite partial to the food too. I've played in Tokyo and Osaka on several occasions and with different types of concerts and I'm going to go back as soon as I can. Japanese people love musical theatre, so I have *Les Misérables* to thank for giving me my chance to play for the fans I have there. I've since played my own solo shows in Japan, and I've also played there with Michael.

It's strange how different the audiences I've played to in Japan are from the ones I've played to in and around Europe or the US. For a start, they initially seem much quieter and calmer. The first time I played my own show there, I was surprised to see people file into the auditorium, almost in silence. In fact, as they sat waiting for the show to begin there was hardly any noise at all. Very different from the rowdy bustle of an expectant audience in the UK or America.

But, once I was on stage and I'd warmed up a bit, they really let go. Suddenly, this reserved crowd were going crazy! They were a fantastic audience to play for.

I suppose the big perk of achieving fame in one field is being given the opportunity to try your hand in other areas of the business. This is why, when the chance arose to do a bit of TV acting, I jumped at it. The role was in an episode of the ITV drama *Mr Selfridge*, in 2013. It had been quite a year for me already. I'd recently completed an eight-city US tour in January, followed by a three-week, fourteen-city tour of the UK. The downside of that was that I was away from the family home in Salt Lake a lot, so missing my family terribly.

In case you didn't see it, *Mr Selfridge* tells the story of the rise and fall of the American entrepreneur Harry Selfridge, who opened the famous London store in the early 1900s. My role as music hall opera singer, Richard Chapman, came about after one of the show's directors, Lawrence Till, put my name forward. For the audition, I had to tape myself both singing and acting, and, as it turned out, they went for it.

Acting for TV was something completely alien to me and, occasionally, I was so into what I was doing, I got completely lost in it all. In one scene, I was performing on stage in the music hall while a scene was taking place on the balcony of the theatre. All the time I was singing, I could hear this murmuring in the background as the actors recited their dialogue. Being a live performer rather than a TV actor, though, I'll often react to something when I hear it. If an audience member says something in earshot, I'll often call back and answer them. So, when one of the actors said something like, 'Oh, this is so wonderful', during the take, I shouted up from the stage, 'Why, thank you very much!'

The director yelled 'CUT!' And everyone stopped in their tracks. 'Right, let's go again, please.'

OK, I thought, *I shouldn't have done that*. I had no idea why it happened; it was just a spontaneous reaction from me being so engrossed in what I was doing. Needless to say, I just stuck to the singing during the second take.

Sometimes, though, you've just got to laugh at yourself. It's very easy, being a classical singer, to fall into the trap of taking yourself too seriously, so I try to avoid it whenever possible. Laugh, and people will laugh with you rather than at you.

Not long after my TV acting debut, I appeared on *The Jonathan Ross Show*, flying the flag for my album *Trust*, which was being released in 2013. My fellow guests on the show that evening were Gary Barlow, Louis Walsh, Stephen Merchant, Nicole Scherzinger and Naomi Campbell. During Naomi's interview, Jonathan brought up the time when she famously fell over on the catwalk in a ridiculously tall pair of platform shoes. After producing those very shoes from under his desk, he suggested she re-live her runway walk in them. But before that, all the other guests on the show would show Naomi their interpretation of a runway walk. Really?

Gary came out on the catwalk first, doing his best sexy male-model walk, followed by Nicole, who was as graceful as anything and, of course, looked amazing. I walked out, wondering what I could do to make the moment memorable. I got to the end of the catwalk, put my fists up in a fighter's stance, and on the way back, purposely tripped over my own feet and fell flat on my face. Naomi came out next and showed us all how to do it perfectly.

She was another of those people who I found to be absolutely lovely. A huge megastar in the fashion world, but such a great personality and a down-to-earth human.

* * *

A few years later, I found myself yet again veering way out of my comfort zone. This time it was on stage, in 2016, on the Broadway show *Finding Neverland*. I was working for the producer Harvey Weinstein, which now feels very strange. The show, which is the story of Peter Pan's creator, J. M. Barrie, and based on the movie starring Johnny Depp, had music written by Gary Barlow and Eliot Kennedy. Barrie was a great character to play; a writer who isn't having much success until he becomes romantically involved with a young widow who has four sons, one of whom inspires his new play, *Peter Pan: The Boy Who Wouldn't Grow Up*. I was genuinely excited about taking on the role, as it was quite different from anything I'd done before. The only thing was, I was taking over from Matthew Morrison. Yes, that's right, Matthew Morrison, the dude from the TV show *Glee*, the incredible professional dancer. In contrast, I am not an incredible professional dancer or anything close to one.

Still, I wasn't too worried after Weinstein assured me that, as I was a singer, they were going to focus more on that side of the role and not to worry about the dancing. The idea was that the dancing aspect of the show would be rearranged to suit my ability, which, as you can imagine, was a huge relief.

The trouble was, I only had about two or three days with the show's director, Diane Paulus, before being thrown in with the resident director and dance captain, and just two weeks to learn a show in which I was on stage from start to finish.

On my first day of rehearsals, the dance captain smiled and handed me a pair of dance shoes. Crap. My heart sank. To my horror, we then proceeded to go through, in detail, every single dance step and routine Matthew had done before me. Despite what I'd been told about concentrating more on the acting and singing side of the role, I had to learn it. All of it. Move by move. Harvey Weinstein had misled me. Shocker.

The dancing element of the production really piled on the pressure. It wasn't like I'd never done choreography before, but nothing that even came close to what was expected of me on that show. It was exhausting, although I certainly got myself fit. The bit I found hardest was coordinating the moves with the singing, and when you have to be in-time and in-sync with all the other cast members, it's doubly hard. My overriding thought was that I didn't want to let anyone down; I wanted to do the part justice. There's always an element of that when I'm performing a role, but when it's just singing I'm a lot more confident and in control of what I'm doing.

Still, I threw myself into it. I listened to the resident choreographer and practised hard, day in, day out, until I started to get to grips with it, marrying up each step with the words and the melodies I was singing. In the end, I felt like it was in my body and I was ready to go – well, as ready as I was ever going to be.

I'd love to say it was all plain sailing from thereon in, but that wasn't the case. During the show, there's a scene where I'm concealed beneath a table, under a tablecloth, along with some other cast members. At a certain point, I was supposed to pull myself through the cloth and come out from under the table with the others in a reveal. Also, the table was quite low, so I had to duck down as I came out. Apart from the fact that I timed the whole thing completely wrong, I also didn't duck down as low as I should have. So, while the other cast members slipped out from under the table with no problem, I shot forward and smacked my head on the underside of the table, almost knocking myself unconscious. Consequently, while the rest of the cast was singing and dancing to the number, all the audience could see of me was a pair of legs sticking out from under a tablecloth.

After a while, I got into the swing of it, but those first few shows were terrifying, trying to remember and navigate all the routines. The funny thing is, once I felt like I'd nailed it, I wanted to do more dancing. I still do. And not just dancing, more acting, more everything. Like most entertainers, I always feel like there's more to achieve. It's a little battle we sometimes have with ourselves, when what we should be doing is enjoying what we have now, where we are, and how far we've come. Constantly thinking about what's next and not living in the moment means we sometimes miss out on the stuff happening right under our noses.

When I look back, I realise that I didn't often take the time to celebrate myself, to sit back and enjoy my success or share it. There were times when I probably should have said, 'Let's go on a family holiday! Let's really go celebrate and enjoy ourselves.' Instead, I'd be thinking, *Right, what's next? How can I improve myself and be more successful with the next project?* I just wouldn't stop. I kept putting the pressure on myself and, in turn, on Sarah. It's something I would come to regret deeply.

CHAPTER 9

LES MISÉRABLES

It would be remiss of me not to mention my other big break and dedicate a chapter to the show that perhaps defined my career more than any other: *Les Misérables*. The day Cameron Mackintosh invited me to audition for the role of Jean Valjean in the show's 25th Anniversary concert, at the O2 in 2010, is a day that will stay with me forever. That day, I was also auditioning for the show's writers, Claude-Michel Schönberg and Alain Boublil, and directors, John Caird and Trevor Nunn. It was a huge turning point for me, and although it meant more time away from Salt Lake, Sarah was really supportive of me taking the job.

'It's the perfect role for you, and you should go for it,' she told me.

I remember going to watch *Les Mis* at the Queen's Theatre before I'd accepted the part and thinking, *This is the role for me. I can see myself up there doing it.*

There was such a lot of work and preparation leading up to the concert – music rehearsals, orchestral rehearsals, costume fittings and last-minute changes. It was a whirlwind, but I was so in love with the music. My favourite songs from the show are probably the prologue – 'What Have I Done?' which is so powerful, also the 'Epilogue' – which is beautifully tender – and the song 'Who Am I?' Of course, 'Bring Him Home' almost goes without saying.

I'd got this idea set in my mind that everything came down to singing 'Bring Him Home' at the O2 show. It was the biggest and most important moment in the entire show for me. It was my moment, and it had to be perfect.

During all this, I went back to the show a few times to see Valjean played by Jonathan Williams, who was the understudy at the time but gave an outstanding performance. The more I saw him do it, the more connected I felt to the character, to his passion, and to his quest for understanding and justice.

I told Cameron, 'If you want me to play the role for the concert, I feel like I need to have played it in the show first. I want to grasp and get a feel for it physically.'

'Fine,' he said. 'Let's give you a two-week run in the London production leading up to the O2 to give you what you need.'

At first, I shadowed Jonathan on stage a couple of times, and I followed his nightly routine at the theatre.

'At this point, I'd go down and see the guys in the chorus room,' he'd say, and I'd track him, following the exact same routine. It really helped get me into the zone before I took on the role myself.

That two-week run, which I did in the midst of rehearsals for the concert, really set me up for the part. I felt like I had a fire in me all through the rehearsal period. I pushed myself to the absolute limit, and I never got tired of singing the music.

At the O2 Arena concert, I performed alongside Norm Lewis, Matt Lucas, Samantha Barks, Nick Jonas and a great supporting cast. I'd never played at the O2 before, but by then, I felt like I was totally immersed in the part. I'd absorbed the role of Valjean completely, and I felt proud of myself, not to mention relieved, for having got there. Throughout the performance, I was in my own little bubble – so captivated by the music, the dialogue and the emotion of the character – more than I ever had been before.

Before my big moment – 'Bring Him Home' – I went down on one knee behind a piece of the set while the company were singing 'Drink With Me' and said my own little prayer to help me get through it. Then I asked, 'Dad, please give me a hand,' which is something I always do before a show. During his life, whenever I asked my dad for a hand with something, he was always there – so I've never stopped asking, even though he's no longer around.

I walked out to the front of the stage feeling protected. I felt like my dad was with me as I sang; that I was singing to him as well as the 19,000 people in the audience. At the end of the song, I kept my eyes closed and, for about thirty seconds, I didn't hear any applause or see the audience on their feet. It was an odd moment, one in which I couldn't quite work out what was happening. All of a sudden, it was as if someone had turned up the volume fader, and the applause just got louder and louder. That was when I looked up to see everyone on their feet. I was overcome by it. At one point, the applause started to die down, but then it surged back up again in another wave. I'm not sure exactly how long the ovation carried on, but I was grateful for it. I embraced it wholly. I even broke character to blow the crowd a kiss in thanks.

Backstage after the show, Sarah was there, along with her father, David, who'd been looking after Gracie at my hotel. There were so many people congratulating me as I walked through the corridor towards my dressing room, but all I could see was my daughter – David had brought her to see me as a surprise. I burst into tears the second I saw her.

Following that night, I played the role in the West End for a five-month run at the Queen's Theatre. Before doing it, I wondered if it might be a bit of an anti-climax after doing that adrenaline-fuelled run during rehearsal for the O2 and the concert itself, but in many ways, it was even better. There was something wonderfully familiar about putting the costume on and getting back into Valjean's boots.

During that run, Russell Crowe came to watch in preparation for his role as Javert in the upcoming *Les Mis* movie. And, talking of that, I got to audition for the part of Valjean in the movie, which I was incredibly excited about. My audition was about two and a half hours long, and during it, I sang the whole show and did all of the dialogue. All of it.

The great thing about *Les Mis* is that as the show moves on and the cast rotates, different actors bring their own interpretation of the material, something new to the table. An actor stepping into the role of Valjean will inevitably do it his own way, as will new actors in the other main roles. I think that's what keeps the show alive and as popular as it is.

In 2013, I was asked about the possibility of my doing the Broadway revival of the show, which was due to open at the Imperial Theatre in New York in March 2014. At the time, I'd just released my album *Trust*, and I was about undertake a UK arena tour, so I couldn't commit to the Broadway run.

Eventually, in August 2015, I did finally take the role on Broadway for a six-month run. For me, though, this was a different version of the show. It was the new 25th Anniversary production, which is different in direction and design to the original RSC Trevor Nunn and John Caird-directed version. There's no revolving part to the stage, which was such a big, iconic part of the original show. This didn't sit well with some fans, who loved those moments, and there was even a hefty petition protesting it. Instead of the revolve, the new version of the show relies more on projections which don't involve such complicated scene changes. It was Cameron who decided the production needed updating for a contemporary audience, and this was seen as a more modern, streamlined production, focusing on narrative rather than spectacle.

This meant that the set was also different, and initially, despite the music staying exactly the same, the delivery and accent was switched from cockney London to northern. I have no idea why, and it felt a bit weird, even as a northerner. Eventually, though, it was changed back. Another new factor was that this new production meant that all my entrances and exits as Valjean changed from stage left to stage right. It was a mirror of what I'd done before. I must confess, I prefer the original RSC version, the one with the famous revolve. It's beautiful. I like the new version too, and I enjoyed doing it, but for me, it doesn't have quite the same magic.

That said, I loved the cast and my time in New York. It felt great being back on Broadway for the first time since *La Bohème* in 2002. I had a comfortable apartment in the Hell's Kitchen area, on 52nd and 8th, which was pretty lively and close to work.

I have to say, New York is not an easy city to be alone in, and despite at least being in the same country as Sarah and the kids, this felt like a world away. At the theatre and when I was working, I was surrounded by people, but outside that, it could sometimes feel quite lonely. Most days, it was a similar routine. I got up, went to the gym, had some lunch and then prepared for the show. Post-show, I might have a bit of supper on the way home at my favourite eatery, Cosmic Diner, which was solid meat-and-two-veg meals with a few good cakes thrown in. Sometimes, I'd maybe have a beer if I had the luxury of the following day off. For a treat, I'd go to Gallaghers Steakhouse on West 52nd Street. That place was old school. Originally a speakeasy opened in the late 1920s, it was owned by a former Ziegfeld girl. In the 1930s, it became Manhattan's first steakhouse and a go-to place for actors and sports stars.

It still has that classic vibe, with red leather seating, a panelled ceiling and a beautiful dark wood bar. The waiting staff wear black bow ties, black waistcoats and white shirts. If I was going after a show, I'd always call ahead to put in my order so they had it ready for me. Sirloin steak on the bone with sautéed broccoli and a baked potato. It was quite the sight walking through the place, with all the meat stacked and hanging on display behind glass, and photographs on the wall of all the famous people who'd eaten there. You can't get much more New York than that.

When you're doing a show on Broadway, you don't really have too much of a social life. I certainly couldn't go out partying while I was performing that particular role eight or nine times a week. I had to preserve the voice! Still, while *Les Mis* is a difficult sing, it's also stamina-building, so doing a run like that really teaches you how to manage your voice.

Despite my lack of partying, I did manage to bag an award during my time there; the WhatsOnStage Award for Best Takeover in a Role (WhatsOnStage awards are for London theatre). But even then, there was no glamorous party, or even a ceremony I could get to – just a short acceptance video followed by a cup of tea and a biscuit in my dressing room. Oh well.

As cold as they are, there's something wonderful about the winters in New York. While I was there for *Les Mis*, the city got hit by a snowstorm with a ridiculous amount of snow falling in a short space of time. The whole of Broadway was closed down because people couldn't get into town, and, for those that were there, it was almost impossible to get around. On the upside, the realisation that I suddenly had a precious Saturday off, free to do whatever I wanted, was a real bonus.

New York is quite magical in the snow. Its long, arrow-straight avenues are blanketed in white as far as the eye can see, with snowdrifts that sit like mini-mountains along the pavements, smothering cars, mailboxes and fire hydrants. Well, it's beautiful for a while at least. As in most big cities, it doesn't take long for all the white to turn to grey sludge and ruin the magic.

Sarah and the kids came out when they could, on long weekends and holidays. They came out for Christmas that snowy year, and because Alfie's birthday is 1 January, we cele-brated on New Year's Eve. We all went outside and bought him a glass of apple cider, so we could toast his birthday and the New Year. Then we watched the New Year fireworks from the window of my apartment.

It felt wonderful having them there with me; there was so much to see and do as a family, and I knew the kids loved being there. The downside was that I was always so terribly sad when they had to leave; it wrenched at my heart every single time. Having them there with me in New York was such a joy, but the first few days after they'd gone were agony. It always took me a few days to find balance again and get back into my routine.

Still, I found my paternal skills came in handy elsewhere. One thing I've noticed about playing the role of Jean Valjean over the years is that you tend to become a sort of father figure within the cast. That's certainly the way it's been for me. It's often been the case that if someone in the cast was struggling or had a problem, they'd end up knocking on my dressing room door and then pouring their hearts out. I'm always more than happy to oblige. It's actually rather lovely to be thought of in that way, to be given that trust by your fellow cast members.

In 2019, there was an All-Star Staged Concert version of the show, with Carrie Hope Fletcher as Fantine and Matt Lucas as Thénardier. For this, we went back into the West End at the Gielgud Theatre. The producers wanted Michael Ball and me to team up, with him playing Javert, particularly as Michael had enjoyed a long history with *Les Mis*, having played Marius in the original production.

This version ran for about four months and then came back to the newly refurbed Sondheim Theatre towards the end of 2020. By then, the pandemic was upon us, so we were playing to socially distanced audiences and limited to a fifty per cent capacity. Unfortunately, after just ten shows, London was put under restrictions that meant we had to close the show altogether.

I've always enjoyed my time working in *Les Mis*, and somehow, I can't imagine that it's gone from my life forever. It's one of those experiences where I can't really think of anything negative that's come out of it. It's given me a lot of success and recognition and I'm forever grateful to Cameron, Claude-Michel, and everybody involved for trusting me with such an important and life-altering role.

CHAPTER 10

BALL AND BOE

If *Les Mis* was one of the first big breaks of the first part of my career, my partnership with Michael Ball has been one of the defining elements of the second part. Friendships within the entertainment industry can sometimes be fickle. You might get close to a person, or a group of people, while you're working with them on a production night after night, but that closeness doesn't always necessarily last. It's just the way it is. On the other hand, I've made some friends I'm certain will be friends for life. One of those people is comedian Jason Manford, who I first met in 2011 when he was hosting a TV show called *Comedy Rocks*.

The show was a mix of stand-up comedy and musical performances. I was invited onto the show to sing 'The Impossible Dream' from *Man of La Mancha* along with Matt Lucas, who I'd performed with in *Les Mis*. However, on the way to the studio, Matt got sick and had to go home, so I was left without a singing partner.

Sitting at the TV studio, just a couple of hours before showtime, I thought, *OK, this isn't going to happen without Matt*. How could it when we'd rehearsed it as a duet? Eventually, the show's producer approached me and asked if I'd be up for performing the number with Jason. Apparently, he'd already agreed to do the song before he knew he'd be singing it with me. The poor guy had to prepare for and rehearse the show, present the show and make it good, and now he had to learn and sing a song at the last minute too. When I popped into his dressing room to meet him for the first time, he was understandably a tad nervous.

'I can't believe I've got to sing with Alfie Boe,' he said. 'It's like doing kick-ups with Pelé.'

As I listened to him go through the music in the dressing room, I made a few suggestions.

'Try that phrase more like this; try this line bit softer.'

The thing I learned about Jason is that he's a real professional and loves to set challenges for himself. This wasn't going to be a problem for him, despite the pressure.

'Let's just go out and have fun with it, Jase,' I said in the end. And that's what we did.

On the show itself, Jason stepped up and turned out a great performance – he knocked it out of the park. And it was a joy singing with him. In fact, if he hadn't stepped in, the whole thing would have been scrapped.

From that night, our friendship grew. During my next

tour, I invited Jason to come and sing with me. He ended up driving to a fair few dates, all off his own bat, where he'd join me on stage and duet 'The Impossible Dream' and songs from *Les Mis*. I think he ended up doing ten shows out of my twenty-date tour.

Jason was passionate about singing and musicals, even though he's more known for his TV work and dynamic stand-up shows. He's gone on to star in shows like *Guys and Dolls*, *The Producers* and even *Sweeney Todd*. I think he's a natural when it comes to musical theatre and we've been close friends ever since doing that first TV show together. He's one of those people who I can rely on to be there for me in tough times, and that's a rare and precious thing.

Gary Barlow is another great friend – it must be a northern thing! He's one of the people who encouraged me to dip my toes into the writing pool and write my own material. Aside from appearing in his Broadway musical, *Finding Neverland*, I've worked on several other projects with him over the years. The first thing I ever did with him was his Big Ben Bash, a specially staged concert in Parliament Square to see in the new year, 2014. We sang 'Don't Stop Me Now' together, with One Direction watching from the front row. Gary is also one of those supportive, encouraging friends we all need in our lives. Ronan Keating and Rick Astley are also wonderful, genuine friends. In fact, what's great about all of the people I've mentioned is that they're not just showbiz pals; they're all guys I can ring up and ask if they fancy coming out for a coffee or a pint.

Sir Ian McKellen is, of course, a legend. I first met him doing a show at Buckingham Palace for The Prince's Trust. I remember spotting him before the show and thinking, *Wow! That's Sir Ian McKellen. I need to go and say hello.*

I walked over to him, smiling and offering a handshake.

'Sir Ian,' I said. 'Alfie Boe.'

'I know you are,' he said in that rich, resounding voice of his.

As we got chatting, I was slightly taken aback by his northern accent.

'Oh, you're from the north!' I said.

'I'm from Wigan,' he said, and from that moment, we immediately connected. Ian is from a different world from some of the other people I've mentioned, but he's a great support and will always come along to my concerts. He's an absolute love and a brilliantly supportive friend.

* * *

My relationship with Michael Ball really started way back in 2007, nine years before our first album together. I got a call from my agent about a new production of *Kismet*, which was being staged by the English National Opera at the London Coliseum, and Michael was to star in it. At the time, I'd just recorded my third album, *La Passione*, a collection of Neapolitan songs I'd wanted to do for ages, and had just spent some time on the beautiful Amalfi Coast in Italy doing some promo stuff for its release – a photo shoot and a video – so I was ready for the next project. And, as I'd always wanted to work with Michael, I happily went up for the role.

It was a fortuitous meeting for sure, but a terrible show.

It was on the first day of rehearsal that Michael and I first met. I remember thinking, this is Mr Showbiz, the nation's sweetheart, and I could see why. Michael seemed like a lovely guy, always with a smile, making everyone around him feel at ease, and as rehearsals kicked off we got on well. Unfortunately, as is well documented in reviews and interviews alike, the production was anything but lovely. In fact, it was an absolute disaster, from the design to the staging, direction and everything in between. Michael and I have both, in the past, spoken about it, but it's very much a part of how we met, so it merits repeating. Although thinking about it is quite traumatic, even now.

When the director of the show falls out with the choreographer early on in the proceedings, it's never ever going to end well. That's just one of the many things that happened on *Kismet*. At one point in the show, the director, Gary Griffin, had the ENO chorus standing in a line along the front of the stage so nobody could see Javier De Frutos's choreography, which was happening behind it. As I'm sure you can imagine, Javier wasn't best pleased.

'Creative differences', as they were called, got so bad that Gary didn't even finish staging the thing before he went back to America.

Set in Baghdad at the time of *The Arabian Nights*, *Kismet* follows the story of a cunning poet, played by Michael, and his beautiful daughter, who falls in love with the young Caliph – played by me.

Given world events at the time, with Baghdad a battle-ground, *Kismet*'s opening scene was in such poor taste that it was ultimately cut from the show altogether. It involved me dashing onto the stage with a Kalashnikov rifle, in full army fatigues, under gunfire, while turbaned bodies and dead soldiers lay strewn around the stage, reflecting the escalation of the ongoing war in Iraq.

'It's hell out there,' I was supposed to scream before the Wazir appears.

'Ah yes, it's hell now, but let me take you back a hundred years ...'

It was so misjudged and vulgar, it's hard to imagine how it got as far as it did.

I'd only done the opening scene a few times when I told them I couldn't do it anymore. I wouldn't do it anymore. It was dreadful.

Unfortunately, the show didn't get much better after that, and the worst part about it was that nobody seemed to be steering the ship.

One of my big scenes in the show was singing the love duet, 'Stranger In Paradise,' with Sarah Tynan. During the song, a huge circular piece of scenery was lowered to frame the two lovers, and when the curtain comes down at the end of the song, I was supposed to hop over the piece to exit stage left. Well, on one particular night, as I stepped over it, the stage crew whipped it up too fast, lifting me off stage along with the scenery. I'd have been on my way up into the flies if I hadn't thrown myself down onto the platform below. I was told later that someone from the crew had been out drinking between the matinee and the evening show, so perhaps hadn't been on their A game. It was just one more illustration that nobody seemed to be taking the show seriously. So, as the run went on, we couldn't really take it seriously either.

It was all such a mess, not to mention unfinished, that the two of us had to pull the cast together and then plot and block the bits of the show that weren't done, just so we actually had a show when the curtain went up.

The reviews were shocking, with the *Guardian* dubbing it, 'ENO's bloody shambles'. Michael later told the *Evening Standard* it was like a cross between 'Springtime For Hitler' and *Carry On Follow That Camel*.

The funny thing is, it sold out. Even after the reviews, people were buying tickets, presumably just to come and see for themselves how appalling it was. It's a shame really. *Kismet* is a good show with an outstanding score by Robert Wright and George Forrest, adapted from original compositions by Russian composer Alexander Borodin.

The only good takeaway from that shambles of a production was that Michael and I formed a strong friendship. A couple of months later in 2007, he invited me to appear on his next big show, Michael Ball at the Proms, where I performed 'Torna a Surriento'.

Michael had been nervous about his show at the Proms. Doing a show that was essentially contemporary musical theatre within the classical format of the Proms was pretty revolutionary at the time and quite brave. In fact, he really broke the mould that year.

As well as my solo performance, we discussed singing together on the show, so I suggested 'The Pearl Fishers' Duet'.

I was excited to rehearse with Michael when with we met up in a Maida Vale studio, but when he started singing his part, something wasn't quite right. It didn't really sound like Michael. It was as if he was singing with a mock-operatic tone.

I gave him a look and said, 'What are you doing?'

'I'm singing operatic,' he said.

'Well ... don't!'

'What do you mean?'

'Well, just sing it like you. Don't sing it like an opera singer. Do it as Michael Ball.'

I guess he thought that as it was a classical piece, he should make his voice sound operatic to match my voice. As soon as he went back to Michael, and we sang together, it was as if somebody had switched a light on. Our voices not only worked together, but they also sounded quite lovely. Having never sung together during *Kismet*, this was the first time we'd duetted, but, as you know, it wasn't the last.

It's funny to think that all of that came out of us doing that disastrous show together. I couldn't have imagined then what great things would come out of it a decade or so later.

The other wonderful thing to come out of *Kismet* was that, down the line, Michael would suggest me for that life-changing role of Jean Valjean. It happened because Cameron Mackintosh had originally called on Michael to play the role for the 25th Anniversary concert. Michael turned it down but suggested me. He'd sung Valjean previously but didn't feel like it was the best fit for him, so told Mr Mackintosh, 'Cameron, Valjean is not my part. But I do know someone who could do it and would be interested. Why don't you come and see *Kismet*? Partly to see what a disaster it is, but mainly to hear Alfie sing and perhaps meet him.'

It was perhaps six months after *Kismet* I first got a call from Cameron, asking if I'd be interested in playing the role. The rest, as they say, is history, and in 2010, I stepped onto the stage as Jean Valjean for the first time.

It was about a year after Michael's Prom concert that he and I chatted about the possibility of doing something together.

'Perhaps some live concerts,' I suggested. 'I think that could be really strong, the two of us together.'

Michael loved the idea but thought we might need a third singer to join us to really make it work – almost like the Three Tenors, but more of a musical theatre version. Around that time, we thought about talking to Josh Groban and to Michael Bublé, but ultimately nothing really came of it. Then, about four or five years later, I called Michael again. I'd just finished playing Jean Valjean on Broadway, and although I'd only seen or spoken to Michael on the odd occasion, I was still convinced the two of us together was a dynamic idea and something we needed to mull over again.

'Remember we talked about teaming up? Well, do you fancy giving it a go, but this time really giving it a shot?'

'Definitely,' he said. 'Let's get our management talking and then we can talk about who else we should get to come on board for some concerts.'

'I don't think we need anyone else,' I said. 'Why don't we just go out as me and you, Ball and Boe?'

'Are you sure we can do it, just the two of us?' Michael asked.

Given our success, it now seems funny to think he would even question it, but I guess you never know, do you?

'Yes, I think we can do it,' I said. 'Absolutely!'

When Decca, my record label of the time, got wind of it, they loved the idea of Ball and Boe. They came on board, signed Michael to the label, and soon after, we were recording what would be the first Ball and Boe album, *Together*. On its release, in November 2016, *Together* went straight to Number One in the album charts.

That first album was a real powerhouse. We wanted to go for it and bring out the hits. Songs included 'Somewhere', 'Music of the Night', 'Anthem' from *Chess*, and, of course, a *Les Mis* medley.

The album was followed by a sell-out arena tour and another album the following year, which also topped the charts. Ball and Boe had exploded.

During the process of making our albums, we'll both come to the table with a clutch of songs, and then we'll get into a studio and sit around a piano with cups of coffee and try them out. We'll hash out various lines, harmonising, arranging as we go, and then listening to how our voices sit and blend together on a particular song. These days, we instinctively know which choruses sound good, how the vocals should be arranged, and where the harmonies should go. If something we're trying doesn't ring a bell for us, then we drop it. It's a very creative process, and we get it done pretty fast.

We do quite a lot of the arrangements ourselves, instinctively. I tend to do harmonies while Michael holds down the melody. When it comes to recording, we have someone who'll help out, making sure it's all musically perfect.

For the latest album, *Together in Vegas*, we worked with Dave Arch, who, among other things, is the musical director and arranger on *Strictly Come Dancing*. Dave was a godsend. A brilliant musician and an outstanding arranger who uses world-class musicians. On the *Vegas* album, Dave was in the studio with us throughout, along with our producer, Nick Patrick, who always oversees and guides the entire process. Between the four of us, we rattled through it fairly quickly. I guess it's a case of four musicians who know what they're doing and are all working towards the same goal of making a fantastic record.

For the first week of recording sessions, Michael and I record the songs with a rhythm section: drums, bass, piano, and guitar. This is what I call the 'groundwork', where we put down guide vocals to get the bare bones and structure of the song down. After that, Nick will go off and record brass, strings, backing singers and anything else going on the track. Pulling together and recording orchestras is expensive, so it needs to be done in full-day sessions, getting it all down as quickly as possible. Once that's recorded, we'll go back into the studio with mixes of the entire arrangement; that's when we'll add the final, polished vocals before it's all mixed. Even at that stage, we're in and out of the studio in a few days, recording about three or maybe four songs a day. I'm happy to say it's a very easy and seamless process. One that I enjoy.

Not that it was always so slick every time. I remember a session during the recording of one of the early albums. We were recording in New York and Michael was in the vocal booth, struggling to get this one harmony line. It didn't matter how many times he went for it, he just couldn't nail it.

We were recording in a studio downtown, near SoHo. While Michael was doing his thing, I stood on a balcony in the sunshine. As it turned out, I was outside the studio for hours, lounging, soaking up the vitamin D and fresh air while he laboured on, trying to nail his part.

In the end, of course, he got the harmony bang on, but by the time I walked back into the studio, he was on his way out of the booth looking somewhat haggard. Everyone else in the room looked equally exhausted – like they'd just come up for air after being underground for a few weeks.

'I think we should call it a day,' Michael said, with a smile. 'Let's go and have some dinner, shall we?'

Michael was fine, of course, but it had clearly been quite an ordeal for all concerned. Except for me. I came away with the best suntan I'd ever had; standing out on the studio balcony for hours.

That's the thing about Michael; he has that perfectionist gene. Most people would have given up during that recording session, or at least taken a break, but Michael is always very determined. All he wanted was to crack it and for it to be flawless, as he always does. It's one of the qualities I admire in him: his determination, his conviction and exuberance in everything he does.

I've never really had an experience like that in a studio, but I did lose my voice in the middle of a performance one night. It was during the production of *The Pearl Fishers* at the ENO in 2010. Prior to the opening of the show, I'd had to do some underwater filming in a ridiculously deep tank – in costume. It was only for a minute-and-a-half sequence of film, but, of course, had to be just right. The tank itself was so deep that I had to have divers with me to make sure I didn't swim up to the surface too fast and get the bends.

Apart from almost drowning a couple of times, the water was heavily chlorinated to keep it clear, so it made my eyes sting terribly, but each time I came up to the surface, the director would be there to meet me.

'Sorry, Alfie,' she'd say. 'We didn't quite get the right angle. Can we do it again?'

You can just imagine the sort of thing I was saying under my breath – well, what breath I had left, that is!

Legally, I was supposed to swim for ten minutes, then shower and change my clothes before starting again. Because that never happened, I ended up spending long periods of time in the heavily chlorinated water, and the results were catastrophic. My body started going into shock; I couldn't see, my skin started to peel off – it was horrendous. Despite all the saline washes, antibiotics and a trip to Moorfields Eye Hospital, where doctors informed me I had burnt retinas from the chlorine, I managed to pull it together for the first and second performances of the show. But I was still as sick as a dog. During the third performance, my voice started to pack in; it was an awful feeling because I could feel it slipping away from me as the show went on. Somehow, I got through it, but following on from that, I had to take five shows out to recover. It was a horrible time.

· · ·

When it comes to choosing the songs Michael and I record for albums, I always try to find things that are a bit left-field; songs that people might not expect us to record. It's not always easy. There have been so many crossover classical and musical theatre singers making albums over the years; everything has been done. So, whenever you do record a classic or something that other artists have already recorded, it's best if you bring something new to the table; try to do it differently.

One of those 'unexpected' songs on the second Ball and Boe album had been featured in the movie *Boyhood*, and had originally been recorded by a Californian indie rock band. The idea came about after talking to Michael's assistant, Andrew Ross.

Left. My first publicity photograph – even today I have the same expression.

Right. Showing off my new clogs with my favourite superman T-shirt on.

Left. My first car – I kept it polished every day, parked up and ready to go.

Above. Panoramic views from my house
in Salt Lake City.

Above left. Two regular early morning visitors . . .
ruining my flower garden as always.
Above right. My boy, Redford, our family dog.

The kids and me in New York's Central Park during my time on Broadway performing in *Les Misérables*.

The children and me at Fleetwood Town F.C. for their first football match.

Above. Proud moment with my good friend Michael Ball at the opening night of *Les Misérables.*

Above. With my very dear friend Shirley Bassey at a performance of *Les Misérables* which she attended.

Above. Gracie and Alfie with me in my dressing room, when I was on Broadway for *Les Misérables.*

Above. Dressed like a penguin to receive my OBE medal!

Above. The flower named after me by Philip Harkness at Chelsea: the Alfie Boe OBE rose.

Above. With my best mate Jason Manford after having a quick brew before we both hit the road.

Above. With the great man himself Tony Hadley who joined me on stage for a duet in Birmingham.

Right. Me and Mr Ball living it up in Las Vegas when we released our *Together in Vegas* album in 2022.

Below. With Wim Hof in the Alps when we had finished filming *Freeze the Fear* for BBC One. It was an experience I'll never forget.

Above left. Myself, my sister Maria and our father on a mountain in the
Lake District after regular hikes every weekend.
Above right. A very young photo of my father holding his first child,
my older brother.

Above. My beautiful mum on her 90th birthday.

A picture taken from one of our regular trips to Las Vegas while doing my residency. Here we're at the Wynn Las Vegas casino. I feel immensely proud to be the father of these two beautiful children. I am so proud of you both, Gracie and Alfie Jr.

'We're looking for a great contemporary song for the album,' I told him. 'Something unexpected.'

'Have you heard a song called "Hero" by Family of the Year?' he asked.

'Yes, I love that song.'

I'd been listening to it for ages but for some reason hadn't thought of it for us. It was perfect, though. Not necessarily the kind of thing you'd expect from Ball and Boe, with its gentle acoustic arrangement, but one of those songs that offered a different flavour. It had an intimacy that proved we didn't always have to sing the powerhouse numbers, and that we could do more emotional and sensitive material. As it turned out, everyone loved the idea, and it went straight on the album.

Whatever it was we were doing, it seemed to be working. By the time of the 2017 Royal Variety – my third time appearing – Michael and I really were riding high. We'd just released our second album, *Together Again*, and it felt like we were in high demand, doing all the big events and taking up space on the sofas of all the chat shows.

In the run-up to the Royal Variety Performance, Michael and I rehearsed our songs and dance routine along with the show's host that year, comedian Miranda Hart. It was a blast. Miranda joined us for the finale, singing 'Bring Me Sunshine' along with a team of dancers, and eventually the entire cast of the show.

It's always a high-pressure gig, the Royal Variety, but it's also very exciting. The line-up that year included Paloma Faith, Seal and The Killers, so we were in good company, and as well as doing our big number at the end, Michael and I were involved in smaller skits and scenes throughout the show. It felt like a great time for us; we were everywhere.

As a duo, went from strength to strength, and the following year's Classical Brits was another Ball and Boe high point. We scooped the award for Group of the Year, and *Together Again* won the popular vote for Classic FM Album of the Year, voted for by the station's listeners. At the ceremony, we performed a medley from *West Side Story*, in honour of Leonard Bernstein's centenary celebrations.

The thing I remember most about winning those two awards was that Michael took them both home. There was only one statue for each category on the night, and he nabbed them. Not only that, but he took home the dummy one that they use at the ceremony to present to the artists. The man took *three* Brit trophies home, two official ones and a false one, while I went home empty-handed. I had to wait six months until they made one for me. (Embarrassingly, I think he was asked to give the dummy one back.)

It's been a lot of fun working with Michael through the years, and, of course, our distinct 'Ball and Boe' characters have evolved over time. Michael is pretty much the bubbly, lively, showbiz persona, while I'm the grumpy, slightly cynical one. Actually, there's more than an element of truth to those characters. Michael has that old-school entertainer energy about him, for sure. He's a true professional. One of those performers who can switch it on the moment he steps on stage, whatever's going on in his life. Jazz hands and all that!

I'm not like that at all. My feelings, good or bad, happy or sad, are usually on show and exposed. Whatever the situation, I tend to say what I think.

We even have different touring habits. When I'm on tour with Michael, he'll often go to a hotel near the venue we have just played in, travelling to the next place the following day. Whereas I like to head straight to the next town or city and stay there, so I can wake up in the place where I'm performing the upcoming show.

The combination of two very different characters works, though. Michael being so bubbly and me being the grumpy one, constantly exasperated by his enthusiasm, makes for a comic dynamic. Consequently, there's a lot of mickey-taking and cutting one-liners, but it's all done with respect and in the spirit of fun! There's no malice or any attempt to make one another feel bad. It's all banter for entertainment value.

Back in the early days, the best laughs always came when one of us messed up a line or forgot the words, or maybe even came in too early on the verse of a song. The sly little looks between us were always very funny, coming completely off the cuff. It's got to the stage now that if we make a mistake, we make it bleeding obvious. We'll pinpoint it for comedy value.

People sometimes ask me whether we really get on, or whether my being mean to Michael is real or just playful. In the early days of Ball and Boe, there were admittedly a few times when we butted heads, times when we might disagree on something: a choice of song, perhaps, or the structure of the live show. I guess it's because we're both passionate about what we do and want every element to be right and the best it can possibly be. But this was in the early days, and back then we were still getting to know one another. Once we'd settled into the way of things, the friendship and mutual respect between us has grown and grown. It's one of those partnerships that works and works well, and as time goes on, it just gets easier and smoother.

So, the truth is, we really do get on. In some ways, we're like brothers. We might take the mickey sometimes, but we have each other's back.

There's still more to come, too. We have another album coming in 2024, and there will likely be an arena tour around that. Watch this space!

CHAPTER 11

A HOME IS HAVING SOMEBODY TO LOVE

The decision to move from Salt Lake back to the UK at the end of 2017 wasn't an easy one but in some ways felt like the only one. I'll be honest, I find it quite hard to talk or write about because, by then, I knew Sarah and I were in trouble. We both knew. We'd had five years of me travelling and living apart from the family much of the time, and with Sarah on her own with the children for longer and longer periods, I felt like things were almost at breaking point.

The fact was, most of my work was on the other side of the Atlantic. So, we thought, *OK! Let's see what England has to offer.* I suppose I felt like we were failing, or maybe I'd failed as a husband. Something had to change in order to pull things back from the brink. Neither of us wanted to split up, and I think we both felt that if we moved back to the UK, we'd be together more of the time. Meanwhile, we could mend what was damaged and then build it back up again. The difference was I was going home, while Sarah was leaving her home along with her friends and family in America. I knew that was hard. She loved the home we'd made there, we both did, so it was never going to be easy for her to leave it, whether or not it was the right thing to do. On top of that, we were going to uproot the kids, taking them away from their friends and school. I couldn't help but feel selfish, as if it was me who was doing all this stuff to make us unhappy. I remember thinking, *I really hope this works. There's a hell of a lot riding on it.*

There were times during that period when I felt like I was flying. Things were going great with Ball and Boe; we'd had two Number One albums, won the Classical Brit award for Best Group, I was having dinner with the Queen and roses named after me. Even better than all that, I had a wife and a family, and we all lived in a beautiful home together.

Despite all that good stuff, I'd had this weird notion swirling around me, taunting me the whole time. It was like the foreboding of a bigger challenge to face. A voice telling me that to become a better person, a better man, I was going to have to face trauma. I can't explain it any more than that, but it was there. I wish I'd known then how fragile everything was, how quickly it could all fall apart in my hands, even as I tried so desperately to keep hold of it. But I simply wasn't prepared for what was to come.

It had been a dream of ours to have that perfect English

house. A house in a gorgeous setting with roses around the front door. Abnash was that house. After we'd first viewed it, I researched the name and found it's of Hindi origin, meaning 'that cannot be destroyed'. It was a beautiful seventeenth-century farmhouse in Chalford Hill, which is a picturesque village in the Cotswolds. It was a wonderful place, with five bedrooms, a cinema room in the basement, and a swimming pool. We felt immensely lucky to have found it.

While we were there, I built a music studio and a gym, but apart from that, the place was pretty much perfect already. Within its eight or nine acres, it also had a self-contained cottage, a tennis court, a forest, a meadow, a rose garden, an orchard, a vegetable garden and a picking garden for flowers. It was the dream, or at least that's how it seemed, and we both felt so blessed to have found it.

Sitting here now, writing this book in a rented flat, it strikes me how much all the rooms, gardens and grandeur meant to me back then; so much more then than they do now. Maybe then, it was all a measure of how well I was doing and how successful, although I'm sure I didn't think of it like that at the time.

Looking back on it now makes me realise how much I desperately want to have a real home again, but the home I'm talking about has nothing to do with the beautiful building or the wonderful grounds or the pool or the cars or any of that. A home for me now is having somebody to love, wherever that is. It's being with a partner and having my children close. It's the opportunity to build memories. It doesn't matter where I live or what the house looks like. In the end, the big house and possessions only satisfy the ego. That's not what life is about. I think sometimes we all need reminding of that.

In the months leading up to the pandemic, despite our seemingly perfect home, communication between Sarah and me was falling down. I'd spent so much time working away that sometimes when I was at home with the family, I felt strangely out of place.

Despite the move, Sarah was still struggling with being on her own with the children and the animals. I knew that, and I couldn't blame her. While she was feeling the strain of taking care of the house and the kids, I was miles away on a stage, making a fool of myself somewhere. Yes, I was working hard, but I was being fed and watered while I did it, driven around from place to place and generally looked after. When you're out on the road, touring or doing shows, you're in a kind of bubble. You don't really have to think about much apart from getting up there and performing every night. The people you're with, your band, your team, or whoever, become your family, your whole world.

Compared to Sarah's, my life was glamorous and varied; I became more and more aware of that as time went on. I was lucky; I had my work and the love of performing. Plus, I had a family to come home to at the end of it. Still, I never took her acceptance of my being away all the time for granted; at least, I tried not to. The truth was, I just didn't know how else to do things. I needed to work, and what's more, I wanted to. The trouble with my chosen work was that it meant travelling and lots of it; it meant hotels and planes and late-night phone calls or FaceTime with the children rather than being there in the home. It was something, as a couple, we had always known and accepted, but gradually, as time went on, it was taking its toll more and more. On both of us.

There was a cycle to it for me. I'd come home from an extended trip away or a tour, and, for a while, I'd feel a little bit strange. When I say I felt like I didn't belong there, I suppose what I mean is I'd lost the rhythm of family life. I'd try my best to fit in, to get into Sarah's routine and the children's routines. I'd try to remember the rules of the house, so to speak. Silly things like reminding myself how to stack the dishwasher properly or the way things were cleaned; all those things I didn't have to worry about while I was on the road where most of it was done for me.

After a couple of sticky weeks, I'd eventually start to fit back in. I'd feel more like I was home and realise, *This is OK. I feel better now.* Then, just about the time when I was feeling settled and really into the swing of being a family man, I'd have to leave again. This was always when the cracks would show, and Sarah and I would be short with one another, or we'd argue. I'd be anxious about leaving, knowing Sarah felt that stress too, and the tension would build.

Still, all the time I was trying to make things work, I just seemed to be making more and more mistakes. Inevitably, by the time I left for the next trip away, there was a certain amount of underlying animosity. I left home feeling rejected and lonely, while Sarah was left frustrated, on her own in the house with the kids. She probably felt abandoned and lonely too.

I have to be honest. This section of my story is blurry in parts and what I do remember is quite difficult to talk about. I think that's what tends to happen with trauma. You block stuff out, but then it can come back to hit you without warning, particularly if it's something you haven't dealt with or worked through, and sometimes even when you have. When that happens to me, when things rear their head again without warning, it can send me into a downward spiral, which is what I mean when I say this is difficult to put down in words.

Sometimes, in order to survive the worst times, I've told myself stories, diluting the truth and changing the narrative to help me get through. I have to stop myself then; assess how honest I'm being with myself and with my own story.

The crux of it is that Sarah and I separated after going through a really rough patch when all the loneliness, frustrations and anger we were both feeling came to the surface. Consequently, I left the family home feeling devastated. This time, I wasn't leaving to work or to perform. I was leaving because we were separating. There was a terrible finality about it.

On the day it happened, I couldn't imagine anything worse; it was the hardest and saddest thing I'd ever had to do. Looking back, it seemed so unreal, like I was watching myself from above; packing a bag, getting into a car and driving away from ... well, from everything. Then, within a couple of hours, I was sitting in a hotel room on my own, heart-broken, screwed up and lost. I wouldn't wish that feeling on anyone.

Our separation threw me off balance. It wasn't just my sadness at the break-up, which was hard enough. It was also the idea that everything I'd thought of as my everyday life was going to change. I was a family man. I had a wife and children that I loved. That was me. It's what I knew.

From then on, everything seemed to snowball. There was so much despair swirling around me it was hard to escape. A negative press article about me, two negative press articles. Anger from Sarah while I stood, desperate to fight my corner. Loneliness and shame at having failed as the head of my own family. All this became a crushing weight on my shoulders and, for the first time in my life, there was nobody I could share the load with.

At the time, I had no idea how little control I had over what was happening. I was a searching for reasons why my head felt like it did, and why all this had happened. Was it all my fault? I thought that because I'd started drinking too much, I could blame everything on that. It was convenient to lay blame at the feet of the social world I was in, and the business I was in, with its drinking and drug taking. Surely, that was why it had all gone wrong.

There were times when I felt like I was being knocked about, like I was somehow being bullied by my own life. As hard as I tried, I couldn't stop the downfalls and the sadness that came at me relentlessly. The more I tried to pull away from it, the faster it came at me. Eventually, it took over me completely. It was all there was.

There came a point where I just wanted to disconnect altogether. It seemed an easier option than facing all the devastation. The layer upon layer of sadness that I couldn't see a way through. I'd been knocking back the drink to stay numb, but now I'd arrived at a place of desperation. I couldn't face what my life had become so I did something drastic. I drank too much. I took too many pills. I had no intention of killing myself. In fact, I don't think I had any intentions besides obliterating the world around me. If anything, I intended to detach, to rid myself of the endless sadness. I never thought about ending my life, but I came dangerously close.

My actions ultimately led to me going into a detox facility in London before being transferred to a rehab facility in Wiltshire. The plan was that I would spend five weeks there trying to build myself up and get back on my feet, which, at the time, felt insurmountable. I mean, how was I supposed to get back to being the person I should be when I didn't even know who that was anymore?

CHAPTER 12

RECOVERY

When I walked into the Nightingale to start my detox, my main feeling was disbelief. I couldn't get my head around the idea of being there, and I couldn't believe this was me. It seemed impossible to associate myself with the situation I'd found myself in, which made it all the scarier. All I wanted to do was go home and get my life back together. But that wasn't an option. My luggage was taken away, as was my belt and anything sharp. Anything that could do a person harm. iPads, phones, computers – they all go, too. All I was left with was the clothes I needed while I was there. That was it. It was tough. I was tired all the time, fighting against the medication I was on and trying to combat all the dark thoughts and feelings that were coming at me. After five days, I was driven out of London to the rehab facility, where I continued and completed my detox.

At first, the idea of being in rehab was alien to me. What I mean by that is, I wasn't sure I met the requirements. Weren't most people who go to a rehab facility battling one or more addictions: drugs, alcohol or any number of other things? They go there to fix themselves, to be fixed, right? It's true, I was there to fix myself too, but I wasn't sure there was any one addiction as such that I could pinpoint. I'd certainly been drinking too much, but was I an alcoholic?

Still, I went through the same programme that everyone went through because I needed it. That, at least, was clear. In going through it, I realised that aside from having problems with alcohol, there were also issues around co-dependency to deal with – excessive emotional and psychological reliance on a partner. I'd had a bit of therapy before, outside of rehab, but for some reason, I never really gelled with any of the therapists I saw and therefore didn't feel like I was benefitting from it at the time.

As I saw it, I was there to fix my head in general. The mind is a strange thing; at least mine is. It can switch from being my best friend to my deadliest enemy from one day to the next. The enemy, peddling doom and gloom, screaming at me that my whole world is an utter disaster, and the best friend telling me in a calm, soothing voice that I'm living my best life. Only, by that point, there was no best friend anymore. The enemy had stormed the building and taken over completely.

It was my management company at the time, Rocket, who'd decided on that particular place. They'd dealt with

artists with addiction problems in the past. For them, this was the best place for me to be. Sometimes, though, I found it hard to put trust in the people making all the decisions for me. I felt like they were telling Sarah one thing and me something completely different. Was I being paranoid? Maybe. Maybe not.

I wish I could say that I'd had any input into the decisions about my care and rehabilitation, but I wasn't up to it. I felt very much out of control. People told me where I should go and what I should do, and I stumbled along with it because I didn't have it in me to resist or even contribute to the discussion. It was as if I was living in a kind of foggy haze, numb and completely paralysed. The thoughts I did have at the time were like an endless, tormenting record playing over and over in my mind. Thoughts of being with my children again, the fear of how life might be without them and Sarah. What would life look like when and if I came out the other side of all this? I certainly didn't have the wherewithal to decide what was best for me.

Clouds House is a rehab facility set in a Grade II* listed building, a large mansion house in Wiltshire. Within the living quarters, there's room for various therapy groups and meetings and a communal lounge with a balcony where people could go out and have a cigarette. It's funny, there were days when I'd stand on that balcony, looking out over the open fields, wondering where I'd end up if I just started walking from that spot and kept on going. Could it be possible to forget all of this stuff and just get lost somewhere for a while?

Luckily, my self-preservation head always took over. I wouldn't have been doing myself any favours by walking away. That much I knew.

Originally, Clouds had been built as a grand family home, but over the years, it had also burned to the ground and been rebuilt, housed wounded soldiers during the war, and been a school. It's been a drug and alcohol treatment centre since the eighties, now run by the Action On Addiction charity.

As nice as it was, though, Clouds didn't feel like one of those celebrity rehabs we've all read about. We weren't exactly roughing it, but I didn't feel like I was living in luxury either. It was pretty but not ostentatious and welcomed people from all walks of life. It didn't matter that I was a singer on television and most of the other guys had so-called regular lives and jobs; we were all there for the same reason. All in the same boat. We were there to get better in whatever way we needed to.

The recovery programme there was based on the twelve-step programme. Within this programme, I was expected to take part in group therapy sessions, plus my individual therapy sessions. There was also the on-site detox that I'd gone through, and where most people landed when they first came through the doors.

The day-to-day routine of the facility came as somewhat of a shock to me. I slept in a single bunk, sharing a room with one other person. Some rooms had three or four beds, so I guess I was quite lucky. It was strange at first, though, sharing your sacred sleeping space with another human being, a stranger. After a while, I found it strangely comforting, knowing I wasn't on my own and that there was someone who'd have my back if I needed them. Actually, I think Clouds had a knack for pairing suitable people together. I was put in with a guy who'd been there for a while, someone who knew the ropes and could teach me what was what.

There were no phones, no tech or electronics, and there wasn't even a TV or music. That was hard for me. Music is such a big part of me, so five weeks without it was like torture. Just like having a TV or a smartphone, music was seen as a distraction. The idea is to just be there with yourself, to sit with yourself and face whatever has brought you there, head-on. Still, even then, there was still music going on in my head. I'd walk around the place singing songs in my mind, and sometimes it felt as though I could really hear them. We could choose a book to read; that was allowed. I read *Treasure Island* because it took me somewhere far away at times when I needed it.

We woke up to the ring of a bell, at about 7am each morning. Then I'd shower, dress and head downstairs for our morning greeting and notes. This is where we'd discuss our thoughts and intentions for the day in our respective groups.

We were all assigned groups, with about six to eight people in each. You can just imagine the broad spectrum of people in each smaller group; they were from all different corners of society and all parts of the country. We all had assignments to write up and hand in, therapy sessions to attend, both one-on-one and in groups. We even had art therapy – there was never a dull moment.

Within the running of the house, we also had what were called our TDs – 'therapeutic duties'. These were the things that certain people in the group felt weren't going to help them with their recovery and therefore resisted. And by certain people, I'm very much including myself in that. As far as I was concerned, I wasn't there to do the housework. What was all that going to do to help me heal?

During the first few days, the stress of what was happening around me and the fear of this place I'd found myself in boiled over. You might call it a meltdown. I lost it; toys well and truly thrown out of the pram. All I wanted was to leave. To walk out, go home, get back to my family and correct everything that was wrong. I really didn't see how being up to my elbows in dishwater might help any of that.

'I'm supposed to be here to clear my head and get myself together, not to mop floors, do the dishes and lay tables,' I announced to several members of the team.

Of course, the staff who work at the facility have heard it all before. My complaint came as no surprise to anyone, and my little freak-out was barely acknowledged. They just looked at me as if to say, don't worry, you'll get it eventually, and then went about their business.

And yes, I did get it, fairly quickly. Without music, TV or other outside stimulation, my go-to was to tidy up and clean, to mop and hoover the floors. I found myself laying the tables for dinner and cleaning up afterwards, and, what's more, as time went on, I started to enjoy it. I enjoyed washing the dishes methodically and running the hoover around. In time, I started actively looking for jobs if I didn't have one, asking for more stuff to do. Though I didn't realise it at the time, the discipline of self-care, of having care and consideration for myself and others and our living environment, resonated. Eventually, I realised that was the idea behind the TDs all along. It wasn't just because they couldn't afford cleaners. It was about us.

When you're depressed or living with addiction or both, it's so easy to sink into a dark hole and let everything go. Dishes pile up, rubbish doesn't go out, and personal hygiene can go to the dogs. You might eat really badly or not at all. You stop caring because you don't see the point anymore. Facilities like the one I was in try to help people see past that bleakness and regain self-respect. Those simple chores and routines are a huge part of that.

It's certainly one of the key parts I took away from my experience. Since I've been living alone, I cook proper meals for myself as much as possible. I keep my flat neat and make my bed every morning. Your surroundings can be a reflection of your state of mind, or vice versa. When one is a mess, the other follows suit. Living like a slob because you feel sorry for yourself just makes a bad situation worse.

That's something else I realised when I first entered the rehab facility; how most people start just feeling sorry for themselves. I certainly did. The tears you shed when you first go into rehab are all about feeling sorry for yourself. Overcoming that was going to be a big step for me.

Each day, once we'd completed whatever therapy we had and finished our TDs, our time was our own. There were newspapers to read, or I could walk in the garden before dinner. There were board games to play and a badminton set in the garden. We were also allowed to walk down the road to a viewpoint, which looked out over the Wiltshire country-side, but only for fifteen minutes, just to get a bit of fresh air and exercise. It was a very pretty view, but one I'd be happy never to see again. There are plenty of other nice views in the world.

That said, much of our downtime was spent sitting around in a circle or group, just talking. These chats didn't have to be a set therapy session; it was something some of us chose to do, continuing the conversation and learning from one another's experiences.

One of the best things about being in rehab was being able to feel that I could speak without judgement. That was a major step forward; allowing me to let go of certain things and open up about the past. There were things I was proud of and things I'd got very wrong. Being able to share all of it, to get it out there without someone pointing the finger and tell-ing me I was a terrible person, was major. I mean, it's not as if I didn't have a low enough opinion of myself already, without anyone else adding to it. I found that kind of group therapy much easier in many ways because the spotlight wasn't solely on me. If I felt like I wanted to stay quiet and hide on a certain day, I could.

The other healthy part of the process was the discipline

of just being there. Throughout my time, I was always aware that I could leave. I knew that if I wanted to, I could go and ask for my bags and walk away. This wasn't a prison and I hadn't been sectioned. A couple of people did collect their bags and leave, but surprisingly I didn't even come close. If anything, the facility became a safe haven for me. The last thing I wanted to do was to duck out before I was strong enough or ready. I realised as the days went on that this was the only place where I felt I could speak my mind, let go of my thoughts and pour my heart out.

Unfortunately, there was one occasion when I was forced to leave the facility because of a work commitment. It's not really the way to do things. I didn't want to go, and, as it turned out, it was a mistake to do so. I got so anxious on the journey there, I had the car pull over so I could throw up. In the end, I did it, but it set me back. I resented having to go, and it wasn't a mistake I would make twice.

After that, I was even more determined to stick it out and complete my time there. It became like one of those challenges I've so often set myself in life. I had to see it through and come out of it a better man. This was the only option, the only good outcome.

I got a lot from the therapy sessions and from the friends I made. That was one of the real surprises for me, making friends in a rehab facility. OK, so I knew I wasn't there to make friends or build a new social world for myself, but I met some remarkable human beings there. Wonderful people. There was a certain privilege in witnessing someone who'd sunk to their lowest point, gradually rise to become the person they were meant to be.

People would arrive in a terrible state, drunk or on drugs, and the transformation was often astonishing. As the days went on, post detox, you witnessed the real person emerge. The empty shell who'd walked through the door suddenly came alive. When you take the drugs, the alcohol, and the addiction away, you begin to see the genuine article. The person who was put on this earth for a specific purpose to contribute in their own unique way. The human being who was underneath all that crap. It feels like a miracle. It's beautiful.

As time went on, I tried to be of use to the people who'd newly arrived, as the guys who came before had supported me. One poor guy came in, a young lad, who was constantly crying; he was in a really bad way. By then, I felt a little bit stronger, at least strong enough to take him under my wing and look after him as much as I could. I noticed over time how he started to settle in and get stronger too. I realised that it was a cycle, but also that the work we were doing in rehab was just the start. Once I left the safety of Clouds was when the real work would start.

Some of the men there were worldly-wise; they had something to say, they were bright and had talents. Like me, they were dulled by their weaknesses and the demons they couldn't say no to.

There was a guy called Joe there who was a huge support to me.

'You'll never regret staying but you'll always regret leaving,' he said of rehab, and he was right.

Joe had suffered from alcohol addiction and also had issues in his relationship. He was a bit younger than me, in his early forties, but he was a real figurehead in the house. He left just before me and has really turned his life around. He was someone to look up to and be inspired by, giving me advice and helping me through some of my dark moments. It was good for me to be able to see the strength he had. Observing other people there made me want to mend, and I wanted to have that strength that I'd seen in Joe.

'Whether or not your marriage to Sarah survives, you have to stay strong, Alfie,' he told me one day. 'Keep your head up.'

I told Sarah as much when she came to Clouds for a therapy session together a few days later.

'Whatever happens, even if we don't make it, I want you to know I'll always be your friend.'

It was hard for her to come there, seeing me in that place. But admitting that to her and to myself was a turning point for me. I was permitting myself to be OK. I didn't have to live life in fear, and there was a way forward on my own. Looking back, things had probably already gone too far with us. Even then, the cracks in our marriage were probably irreparable, but we'd just kept going and trying.

One of the things I've learned through all this was that I had been sad during the last couple of years of my marriage, depressed even. I hadn't wanted to face it, but now I knew it to be true. There were times when I'd been on top of the world, and others when I was frustrated because I felt like I wasn't getting it right and that Sarah was angry with me. Even when she wasn't, my head told me she was. Over time, it broke me and left me with depression. Realising that and admitting it to myself was a real breakthrough.

I spent Father's Day at Clouds, which was really painful. I was a father, yes, but where were my children? They'd sent me flowers and made me a card but I couldn't be with them. They also sent chocolates, which were taken from me because they went against the diet that had been set out for me. The rules were strict, and while they were all there for good reason, it was hard.

There was an older guy at the facility, George. He was someone I befriended and admired. He was comical, a larger-than-life character. On his first day in detox, he walked in, still off his face, and said to me, 'You're definitely not the first person I thought I'd see in here!'

George was a bit of an old hand. He'd been in rehab three times and had suffered through addiction. I admired that he hadn't given up and was still giving it another shot. Seeing him made me wonder if I had it in me to go through this process over and over. Once was hard enough.

I was never clear on what sort of life George had outside the facility or what his social circle or family was like, besides knowing he had a brother. From all I could fathom, he struck me as a lonely guy. Someone who very much needed the social aspect of rehabilitation. He loved to engage and talk with people and to make them laugh. As it turned out, he also enjoyed a sing-song.

I'd gone into rehab armed with a guitar, but I wasn't allowed to play it or even keep hold of it. Off it went to a safe lock-up, probably saving my fellow housemates many hours of me strumming away, crooning sad and depressing songs. There were, however, Friday nights, when I was allowed to collect my guitar and play it.

On those nights, I'd play and sing songs in one of the therapy rooms for anyone who wanted to join in. Usually, someone would pull out some percussion instruments from our music therapy sessions, and there'd be someone shaking a tambourine or tapping a bongo. It got to be quite the unexpected little jam session.

On one of our more boisterous singalong evenings, George insisted that we do a duet together. I admired his confidence. We ended up doing Queen's 'Bohemian Rhapsody' in front of the whole group. It was quite a moment, everyone watching and listening as our voices filled the room. It was a flicker of light during a dark time, a light-hearted detachment from the stress and pain. It's something I'll never forget.

Sadly, George didn't make it back out into the real world. He was one of the unfortunate ones who stumbled and fell again once they'd left the facility. Unable to cope with life, some get lost or tempted again, dipping their toes in the water only to get bitten. In George's case, it ended in tragedy.

Months later, at an AA meeting, someone told me that he'd died. It was a real blow and hard to take in and get my head around. George was someone I'd lived with, sat at tables and had meals with, talking and laughing as we ate. Someone I'd got to know and shared my struggles with, as he'd shared his with me.

I remember feeling excited for him and others about what was next in their lives and what their futures held once they got out of the facility. You do: you get involved with the people and their stories, and you desperately want that happy outcome for them. The same happy outcome you wish for yourself. When you hear that someone has overdosed, it's pretty devastating. All that hope and excitement you had for them, smashed in an instant.

I grew to have such fondness and love for those people and for some of the people I've since met at meetings. They're people who simply needed help but didn't know how to ask for it. Throughout my experience, I've heard people say addicts help addicts, and I believe that's true. It's helping each other through whatever it is we need to get through, simply by shared experience, listening and empathy.

Outside of that supportive environment, I'd often found that people were more interested in advising before they'd heard the whole story, or talking over me to compare my woes with their own. There were times when I'd confide in someone about a problem and they'd jump in and say, 'Oh yes, it's the same for me ...' before going off on something completely irrelevant to what I'd been talking about. Only now the conversation was about them, and I'd end up listening to their problems.

I'm at a point now where, when talking about anything important, I try to take my time. I want to slow down and think about exactly what it is I'm about to say. Usually, I'm working from the emotion I'm feeling at the moment I'm saying it, so it's vital to be clear on things. When somebody jumps in with advice before I've even finished a thought, it's not helpful. I end up thinking about what they're saying before I've finished my own thought process, and they're already giving me advice after hearing only a fraction of the story.

It's a similar thing when talking about depression and feeling low or anxious. When you broach subjects like that, people often look for something to solve immediately.

'What is it you're depressed about? What is it that's actually getting you down? What's making you anxious?'

For me, that's when frustration kicks in because often, it's near impossible to pinpoint exactly what's bringing you down, and it probably isn't just one thing anyway.

In rehab, I found that most people were ready and willing to listen. I think probably because there was often something to learn from the shared experience of a person with similar struggles. The people there didn't feel like they had all the answers, so they listened carefully in the hope of finding some.

Learning to get things out of my head and off my chest helped me the most during rehab. Finding alternatives to drinking or wallowing was the key – talking, exercising, cooking food for myself, having pride in my surroundings, and, of course, talking. These were the things that would hopefully keep me afloat and give me a fresh perspective. Maybe save my marriage.

All through it, I hoped to rebuild my relationship with Sarah, and that's what I tried to do. To me, this was everything. My marriage and my family were the foundations that everything else was built on, and I was sure Sarah wanted with all her heart to make things work too.

By the time I felt ready to leave, Sarah had agreed to give things another try and allow me to come back to the family home. Of course, I was happy, but it was tough. For a start, being out in the world reminded me how fast it moved. After strolling around the grounds of Clouds for five weeks, taking my own time, walking through the streets almost felt like a brand new experience, with everything going super-fast around me.

I felt shame about what had happened to me and I felt awkward being around our friends again. Some friends even distanced themselves, and ultimately I lost them. On the upside, real friends made themselves known, and I'm forever grateful to them.

Down the line, I wrote a song called 'When Nobody's Watching', which talks about some of the things I went through behind closed doors leading up to my time in rehab and beyond. It's about allowing myself to be vulnerable and weak in private in order to be able to function when out in public or in the company of others. It's about taking my own private time to fix myself in order to get better and stronger for the future.

• • •

What I've learned is that we never really know what's going on behind somebody's smile, the facade they show to the world. I've sometimes met people who I'd have probably described as happy, bubbly characters only to find that underneath the jolly exterior, they're drowning. That idea of 'putting on a brave face' is something I've often struggled with. I'm definitely not someone who can do that. Usually, my feelings are very much on show. Don't get me wrong, I'll do my best to carry on with what needs to be done, but with me, I think it's easy to tell when something isn't right. And while it's admirable when a person can keep smiling and carry on when things in their life are tough or crumbling, I don't think it's necessarily the best way to handle things.

It's always shocking when we hear of somebody who's taken their own life. Quite often, even the people closest to them don't see it coming.

Last year, there was an exhibition on the South Bank called The Last Photo. It was launched by suicide prevention charity CALM, and featured photos of fifty smiling people, taken in the last days of their lives, just before they'd taken their own lives. It was quite something to see. Most of the people, smiling happily in their photos, looked like they were loving life, but what was going on underneath was something entirely different. The exhibition also shared the stories of shock and terrible heartbreak their friends and families experienced. Seeing it really made me think about what a strange illness depression is. So hard to pinpoint and assess, especially when you hear about it from someone who's been successful in the entertainment industry. Someone who we might think has the world at their feet.

That's why I think the masking and burying of our struggles and issues isn't healthy. Our mental health is just as important as our physical health, more in some ways. We have to be able to talk about stuff. We have to be honest with ourselves and others and let it out.

With me, it's still a day-to-day thing. This morning, though, as I'm writing this, I feel pretty good. It's a bright morning with the sun breaking through, I slept well and I feel refreshed. Later, I'll go outside and treat myself to a nice lunch somewhere. It's little victories. It's one foot in front of the other and one day at a time.

CHAPTER 13

END OF A MARRIAGE

As tough as rehab and the readjustment were, for now I was just happy to be home and with my family. It had been a truly terrible time, but hopefully, it was over. The only way was forward. Then it came: a worldwide pandemic. Suddenly, we were living in the upside-down. You turned on the news and there were people who were fine one minute, in the hospital the next, and tragically gone the day after. The only security people had was that if they were young and healthy, they were less likely to become seriously ill with Covid-19. And then suddenly, we weren't even allowed out of our homes anymore. The world had literally shut down.

It's a strange thing; as scary and uncertain as it was, there was some novelty value during that first lockdown, don't you think? None of us knew what was going on, or how things were going to play out. We just had to keep watching the news and get on with it.

Mercifully, none of our family caught Covid during those first uncertain months. Sarah and I were at Abnash with the kids, doing the same things everyone else was doing – making bread, spending time together as a family, watching too much television and, of course, home-schooling.

Eventually, the novelty wore off for most people; we all started to feel trapped. The people running the country didn't seem to know what they were doing any more than we did. Life suddenly felt a bit more difficult, more uncertain.

That was definitely the case in our house; by that point, both Sarah and I were really feeling the strain. There just didn't seem to be any way forward or room to breathe. Through lock-down, like most people in the entertainment industry, I felt anxious and stressed. So much was unknown during the pan-demic. There was a long period when every concert hall and theatre in the world was closed, and pre-vaccine, we couldn't know for sure whether they'd ever be able to open again. We hoped, we believed, but we didn't know.

After a while, the pressure of not working got to me. My head just took over, and I felt lost again. I wasn't even sure who I was without my work, without music and performing. I started worrying about our finances and what a future with-out work might look like.

The only thing that took me out of those negative thought patterns was to sit down and create, to write my own songs. It was something I started to enjoy and was such a great tonic.

Not only was I being productive, but it was soothing for my troubled head, getting those thoughts and feelings out and turning them into music.

When travel restrictions finally relaxed a little, I had the opportunity to do some writing and recording over in France, with a songwriter called Simon Climie. Simon had been one half of eighties pop duo Climie Fisher, but also penned songs for Pat Benatar, Eric Clapton and Rod Stewart, and wrote the classic hit, 'I knew You Were Waiting (For Me)' for George Michael and Aretha Franklin, along with his long-time writing partner, Dennis Morgan. When I first thought about writing my own material, Simon was the first writer I approached. I was introduced to him by my new manager, Craig Logan. They'd been pals for a long time – Craig was the bass player of eighties pop band Bros, who were having hits at the same time as Climie Fisher.

I probably shouldn't have even considered going really. It hadn't been that long since I'd come out of rehab and back into the family home. Sarah certainly didn't think I was ready to jump back into work, but I was desperate to do something.

What made it worse was that this all came about pretty fast. So, as was often the case, there was the prospect of me leaving at the drop of a hat. It was a tough few days for Sarah and me. We'd been living at home as a family through lockdown, but suddenly the prospect of me taking off again loomed large over the house. I felt like I needed to get back to my working life and to do what I did best. Meanwhile, Sarah was looking at the prospect of being on her own again. She just saw us falling back into the same old routine, and a part of me knew she was right. In the end, though, I made the decision to go, and that's really when things between us fell apart.

It's ironic really because things between us crashed down when we'd been in a relatively good place. With the France trip came Sarah's feelings of being abandoned and my feelings of being misunderstood and pushed away. As much as I knew how much she hated my being away, I resented feeling guilty about accepting work that involved me travelling and doing what I love. These were not new problems. They were the same issues that had affected our relationship before my stint in rehab and the lockdown. For a while, they'd been pushed out of sight; camouflaged by everything that was going on in the world. The pandemic had been a glue that held us together, but now it was coming to an end, and the old residual feelings were shooting up through the dirt like garden weeds.

At the end of the day, these feelings amounted to the same thing for both of us. Loneliness. Sarah was lonely while I was away, and I felt shut out when I came home.

The writing sessions took place at Simon's place in Villefranche, which is a pretty town near Nice. As we were between lockdowns it felt very nice to be out in the world, despite everything. The sessions themselves were productive, and we were getting stuff done, but ultimately nothing solid came of it. I'm not sure my heart was fully in it anyway. As much as I'd wanted to go to France, there was a heaviness in me the whole time I was there, a fear about what I was doing to my marriage and my family. Instead of enjoying the process and the blossoming of a new work situation after so long in lockdown, I just felt very low again. I'd wanted so much to make a fresh start after I'd come out of rehab, we both had, but it was hard to see how certain things were ever going to change or be resolved.

I don't know why I fell apart the way I did. I loved Sarah so much, but somehow, the connection had been broken. Mistakes were made, resulting in my looking for support elsewhere and telling my troubles to someone I shouldn't have instead of talking to Sarah. Hurting her like that broke my heart, but it resulted in us separating.

It's true, our marriage hadn't been perfect, but rather than facing the problems, I'd ignored them. We'd both put our heads down and carried on for the sake of our children, not thinking about what the consequences might be. For my part, I was weak and made some terrible mistakes. I'm bitterly sorry for every one of them.

Even then, the prospect of living outside the family unit seemed unimaginable, even though I'd sometimes felt so lost and sad within it. Now, I'd have to get used to living a separate daily existence from my kids. It was a tough truth to face, but I had to get myself into the frame of mind where I felt I could deal with it. I had to accept what was happening, accept the change, and realise that I could still have a relationship with my children, even though it was different from the one we'd had before.

CHAPTER 14

BEING ALONE

I still feel it some days, even now. This weekend, for instance, I've felt lonely. It happens sometimes, and I just have to ride it out when it does. Looking out onto the little terrace of my apartment, I'm thinking about the home I left behind, with its lovely big garden; memories of my kids and me, out there in the sun. It's so alien to me, all this. And just when I think I'm getting used to it, I'll hit another bump.

When I feel low, motivation can be a struggle. I wonder how many people reading this have felt the same. Some days, I'll spot some dust on the carpet or marks on the kitchen floor and I'll wonder, how long will that be there? How long will it be till I can't stand it anymore and hoover it up? I thought I was doing OK, looking after myself, but over the last couple of days, I've been anxious, and yes, lonely. I know it will pass, and I'll be OK again soon, but right now, the realisation that it's just me is really starting to sink in.

After we'd finally separated in 2020, Sarah wanted to relocate back to Salt Lake. I understood her reasons. It was where she'd grown up, her family were there, and for her, there was security in all of that. As well as that, Grace wasn't happy with the school she was at in the UK. Her eagerness to head back to America became clearer by the day with all the pictures of charming houses in Salt Lake and California she kept texting me.

I didn't want to be that guy who says to his ex-wife, 'you can't go home, you've got to stay so I can see the children', but at the same time, I wanted to see and be with my children as much as I possibly could. I sometimes do regret letting them go so easily for that very reason.

I bought a house in Salt Lake, and Sarah and the children travelled to America. I would follow on once I'd sold Abnash. That was my next task, packing up our beloved home, and putting it on the market. It wasn't an easy or enviable one.

When the packers arrived, we started stripping things down and taking things to pieces. I watched as our pictures came down from the wall, photographs that told the story of where we'd been and what we'd done together as a family. Each piece of furniture seemed to hold a memory – where we bought it, how we chose it together. Some of the paintings and pictures that we'd collected over the years felt particularly poignant. A vintage travel agent poster about sailing to Alaska was one of the first things we bought together, from a shop in

San Francisco, where we first met. It might not have been high-end art, but for us, it had been quite expensive at the time, an investment.

It was like watching the life and world I'd known being dismantled and then put into boxes and taken away. Worse than that, the person I'd built and created that life and that world with was no longer there with me. I was doing this on my own.

Strangely, I think packing up the kitchen was the hardest for me. The memory of a hundred family dinners dancing through my mind, so many celebrations and great meals, so many dinner parties and so much laughter. I remember thinking about how things can change so quickly, how life can change so quickly. I wondered if these changes, these surprises, were supposed to make me stronger. I hoped they would, eventually.

It was so tough getting rid of those things we'd shared as a family. I sold our cars and the furniture we no longer had use for, and then I shipped everything else over to Sarah. Thank goodness for our gardeners, Heidi and Darren. They'd helped us look after the grounds of that beautiful place ever since we bought it, and after Sarah left, they were wonderful. I think they could see the pain I was in and how hard it all was for me, so they helped me pack everything and then organised the shipping and transport. They took me under their wing at what was a really tough time. They even organised the shipping of our pets. That was hard. It didn't seem that long since we'd brought them over to start their new life in England, and here I was sending them back again.

In the end, everything went, and when the dust settled, I found myself sitting alone in an empty house, which, as I'm sure you can imagine, was not a nice feeling. The house, once full of life and energy, of music, food and laughter, was now empty and silent. There was nothing.

This was a real low for me, and I became very depressed. It was such a struggle getting through every single day, just sitting there waiting to sell the empty shell of a house. It was horrible; there are no two ways about it. My family had gone off to start a new life and I was living in limbo. I wouldn't wish the way I felt then on anyone.

As much as I knew it was happening, I found it difficult to believe what my life had become and where events had led me. I kept saying to myself, *You're not the only person who's gone through this, Alfie; other people get divorced, other people suffer this and somehow get through it.*

I suppose the proof that my time in rehab had worked was that I didn't go down the same road that I had before. Yes, I was terribly sad, but I didn't sink as far. I didn't risk my life. I never realised it at the time, but rehab had prepared me for an existence living alone. It gave me the tools to deal with something that was probably inevitable.

Still, this was a strange time; like nothing I'd ever experienced. Most days, I'd get up and make myself a coffee, put a cardigan on, wrap myself in a blanket and then head into my garden. There I'd sit, for hours and hours, just staring across the garden looking at the scenery. Sometimes, I'd sit there for so long, it was as if I'd become part of the landscape or a piece of garden furniture. There, with my hair growing longer and my beard getting bushier by the day, all I needed was a pointy hat and a fishing rod or wheelbarrow, and I'd have been the perfect garden gnome.

I suppose a lot of us got that way during Covid. We weren't going anywhere or seeing anyone, so what was the point of getting dressed up? Also, I wasn't too fond of sitting in an empty house; there was nothing in there for me anymore. The garden seemed like the perfect place to hang out and bide my time.

Aside from the feelings of loss and sadness, I was also scared. I had no idea what my existence might look or feel like from then on. Breaking up with someone I'd been with for twenty years, the idea of not being with that person day after day, was so hard to get my head around – especially because I still loved her. What was life going to look like now?

At that time, I didn't even know where I'd end up living or what my relationship with my kids would be like going forward. I didn't even know how close we'd end up, geographically. Everything was uncertain.

There was also the nagging fear that I might not be able to work again. I know many people had that kind of fear during Covid, that nothing would ever be normal again. Watching the news, the impact on most parts of society was bad enough, but there'd been such a devastating impact on the entertainment industry. There were times when I wondered if things could ever be the same again, if it could ever bounce back. Would I still get the opportunities and the work I did before the world fell apart?

I'm sure if I'd been in better shape mentally, I'd have been a bit more logical about the situation, but I was feeling very insecure. Left alone to wrestle with my mind, the doubts and fears marched in and set up shop. They festered and ate away at me. I was a mess.

I wasn't even sure how easy it would be to fly to America, with travel rules and restrictions changing by the day. I did everything I could to avoid scuppering any travel plans I might have. I'd had my vaccine, I got the booster, and I tried to avoid being around too many people, which, to be honest, wasn't difficult at that time.

Some friends were naturally supportive, but a couple of others gave advice that felt brutal and difficult to take. I knew they meant well, but sometimes their timing was way off. The last thing you need when you're that low is people doling out what they see as 'tough love' which ends up knocking you down even further.

Others could be quite dismissive. There was one particular phrase that cropped up several times when a person didn't quite know what to say. 'It is what it is!'

I mean, what was I supposed to say to that?

'Oh yes, you're right! I feel so much better now you've pointed out that "it is what it is".'

It just doesn't mean anything, and, at the time, felt very dismissive and hurtful.

I feel like I lost a lot of friends when Sarah and I separated. There were people I thought would be there for me who weren't. What hurt the most was the judgement that came from some quarters. Some people formed an opinion about what had happened without really knowing the truth. Of course, being in the public eye doesn't help. There are inevitably times when certain sections of the media painted a picture that wasn't genuine, and that's hard to take. Newspapers can be ruthless sometimes. I sometimes wonder if the editors of certain publications stop to consider the power they have to make, break or destroy a person. Still, I guess we all have to pay the bills and make a living, even if the job you're doing is contributing to the downfall of others.

With all that said, I was fortunate enough to have a few good friends who were fully there for me. Jason Manford was always on the end of a phone. He checked in on me daily. In fact, Jason was the only visitor I'd had during my stint in rehab. While I was there, he'd drive two hours to visit me, which is something I'll never forget.

The process of selling Abnash took several months leading up to Christmas, but it felt longer. All I wanted was to get it sold so I could spend Christmas with my family, which is ultimately what happened. When it was all done and dusted, I packed up my possessions and followed my family to America. I went because I had to be close to the children, but I knew that in doing that, I'd eventually be living on my own out there. For the time being, though, I was staying with Sarah and the kids at their new place.

As you can imagine, having just separated from Sarah, me living in her basement in Salt Lake wasn't exactly ideal. I had to find an apartment. As much as I wanted to be close to the kids, I needed to give Sarah her space. Eventually, I got a place downtown and moved in for the next year.

Now I was separated from everything familiar to me and everything I loved. I felt lost. Lonely. I was in shock, grappling with the idea that my life could have swung from one extreme to the other almost overnight. Well, that's certainly how it seemed. The pain of not living in the same house as my children was overwhelming, as was the loss of the person I'd loved and lived so closely with for so long.

I know many people who go through separation or divorce after a long-term relationship can relate to these thoughts and feelings. You spend years in a home with a person you care for; years of waking up and seeing your children running around, getting ready for school; years of eating together, watching telly together at the weekend, laughing and playing together. Then suddenly, it's all thrown into turmoil. It goes up in the air and comes crashing down, and when the dust settles, everything is broken. Nothing's the same anymore. The days are no longer filled with all those things. So you have to find a new way. You ask yourself, how do I get through a day without all that? How do you navigate the sadness you wake up with? How do you turn it around and fill all those empty hours? What is it that you need to do to continue living that day?

All this came when I didn't even have work to distract me. I was missing that side of my life, too. The joy of getting up on stage and entertaining. Nothing was coming in, and for the first time in a long time, I was starting to worry about my financial situation.

The apartment building that I was living in didn't help matters. Don't get me wrong; it wasn't a bad place. A two-bedroom flat in a modern building with a large kitchen living area and a nice little balcony. There was also a shared swimming pool on the roof and a gymnasium. The only trouble was, the building itself was a bit of a party hub. The tenants were mainly young business types who liked to get drunk and go for it at weekends, making loads of noise and causing havoc in the rooftop pool. I felt like the oldest person in the building (and I probably was).

Living in a place like that, in an environment where it was all young people crashing around and enjoying themselves, only compounded my sense of being alone. I'd see them at the pool and think about hanging out with my kids in my own house. I remember thinking, I'm a family man. I don't belong here. It felt like such an extreme change.

With work being thin on the ground, I was desperately trying to find things to keep myself occupied. I got up in the morning and went to the gym. I'd do school runs in the morning or pick the kids up after school. If I had nothing else going on, I'd go on day trips, riding my motorbike out into the mountains. In the evenings, I'd go to the grocery store, then come home, cook myself a meal and then watch a bit of television. It was a very ordinary existence in what felt like an extraordinary time, not only in my world but the world in general. I lived for the weekends when I'd have the children over to stay.

I knew they were suffering through all this. The transition was hard for them too. When they were with their mum, they had all their stuff around them, and their rooms were set up – it was home. As much as I tried to make my apartment comfortable, it never felt like home to them. I tried my best to decorate their rooms and put things in they'd like, but it just wasn't the same. It was hard to see because they're both good kids and I knew they were trying. I'm very proud of the way they've adjusted to such a big life change. Sarah and I still get on, and we've always had their best interests at heart, which I think has helped smooth the way. I want Sarah to be successful and happy. I want her to find someone new, and I know she wants the same for me. Having that connection makes life easier for our kids, knowing we both still care.

I hadn't wanted to separate, and I certainly didn't want to be divorced. Still, it hadn't always been the easiest of rides with Sarah and me; we'd had our ups and downs and our struggles. After two decades as a couple, we'd been through so much. My career blossomed and grew during the time we were together, and the support Sarah gave me was a major factor in my success. You can't just throw away those years and those memories and the feelings we had for one another. As well as being a couple, we've always been good friends.

So now, having come through it all, I don't look back on our marriage as a failure. It ran its course. It lasted as long as it was meant to last. We had all those great years together and two beautiful children, which is no failure in my eyes. I miss her, though. Even now. I miss what we had, and I probably always will.

CHAPTER 15

HELPING MYSELF MOVE ON

Music is a great healer. I truly believe that. After such a long period of heartbreak, I gradually realised the need for change and that it had to come from me. I had to do something for myself, and the thing I did best and loved to do was make music.

I went back to writing songs again, and with these new songs, I was able to write lyrics about my past, and how I felt about myself and what I'd been through. It was all a process, but there came a point when I realised that I was no longer feeling sorry for myself. I wasn't completely out of the woods, but at least I was making the effort to move forward.

Some of the songwriting sessions I did during this time were on Zoom calls. That seems to be the way almost everything was done during the worst eighteen months of Covid, but it worked well. I'd team up with various writers online and we'd talk about life, the people in our lives, the things we'd experienced, and specifically what I'd recently gone through. We'd hash out good angles for songs and titles, and, as the songs were ultimately going to be for me, the mood and direction of them would very much be dictated by how I was feeling on a particular day. I still had challenges, and I was still feeling pain, so on the days when those things were prevalent, I decided that writing a song about it was the best way forward. I wrote every day. Some things became complete songs, and others remain ideas or soundbites for the moment, but yes, I clearly had a lot to get out of my system.

One of the writers I worked with is a young guy called Nick Bradley. I wrote several songs with him; he's got this energy and positivity that I remember having when I was his age. Working with Nick helped me engage with that energy again; it opened up so much in me, and I'm incredibly grateful for that.

The big change for me was that instead of listening to and feeling other people's songs, I was now writing my own. Now, I was singing my own story, putting my pain down with the melodies. This, to me, was like self-help, because now I was actually writing the music that was healing me.

One song from this time was 'Saving You', written when I decided I needed to change my actions and behaviour towards Sarah. She'd done a lot, trying to make me feel better about the situation we'd found ourselves in and about the past, while I'd been turning up at her door in pieces, heartbroken that we weren't together anymore. When I wrote this, I was in a place where I felt it was my turn to be strong and that I should be the one doing the saving. Now it was my turn to make her feel better, to be there when she needed saving.

That was such a big breakthrough for me, the realisation that I needed to stop crying on Sarah's doorstep; putting my pain on her. I still loved her so much, but sharing my hurt and pain made the situation even harder for her. I didn't want that. Now, it was time to show her that I'd be OK and that she could be too. It was time to turn my life around and do something positive. To act instead of merely reacting.

I was gradually dragging myself out of the deep hole I'd fallen into, physically as well as mentally. I started exercising and eating healthier food, I started looking after myself. Before I knew it, I was building a positivity which was growing by the day. It was the spark I needed to be able to carry on, to move forward. I started seeing some of my friends in Salt Lake City again – getting out and about – although I had no interest in dating or getting into another relationship. Mostly, though, I kept throwing myself into my rekindled love of songwriting.

'If You Don't Love Me Like That' is about acceptance and change. It's a song I didn't write the lyrics for but worked on with Los Angeles-based artist, Wrabel – Stephen Wrabel, to give his full name – who's a gay songwriter and promoter of LGBT+ rights. I was drawn to the song because the lyrics seemed to reflect my situation with Sarah. The lyrics of the verse ask whether homes, money and possessions are enough to make someone happy. I suppose it's essentially a song about fighting to save a relationship, trying to do anything to make it work, but also acknowledging that if someone is no longer in love with you, you have to move on.

I also spent a lot of time travelling back and forth from Salt Lake to Los Angeles, collaborating with songwriters. I guess it felt different this time because although I was leaving my family behind in Salt Lake, I wasn't living with them anymore. Maybe I was becoming accustomed to not being part of their daily lives. As time went on, I'd put together a really strong body of work, some great songs. I couldn't wait to get them out into the world. Unlike many of the songs I'd performed before, these resonated with me because I'd had a hand in creating them. I'd put down the words myself, and the lyrics seemed to reflect all the different parts of me and what was and had been going on in my life. In fact, many of the lyrics I put down acted almost like a journal of how I was feeling day-to-day.

On the day I wrote 'Start Somewhere' with LA-based Scottish writer Stuart Crichton, I'd had a phone call from Sarah that didn't go well. It was general family stuff, issues with the kids and the like. I guess we were at a stage where everything was still very much up in the air and uncertain, and we were both desperately trying to find our feet. Anyway, that call came on one of those days when I found it particularly hard to take, so I decided to walk to the studio rather than take a car. The thing was, the house where the studio was based was about twelve miles from where I was staying.

Consequently, I walked all the way down Sunset Boulevard, through Laurel Canyon, and down Ventura Boulevard. Halfway up Laurel Canyon, I remember thinking, *I can't take this anymore; I just can't deal with the stress*. I was falling apart, not wanting to feel anything. There's a line in the song about taking my heart out of my chest, putting it in a box and leaving it by the side of the road, which would leave me numb – which is exactly what I felt I needed.

Finally, I got to Sherman Oaks. By the time I knocked on the studio door, I was drenched with sweat from the summer heat, looking tired and haggard. Stuart opened the door and looked at me, wide-eyed.

'Are you OK, Alfie?' he said.

'I'm fine,' I said, despite not being.

Then I had a cup of coffee, sat down, and poured my heart out into the song lyrics.

I suppose you could say it's a song about finding a new starting point. For me, it was the realisation that I couldn't go on as I had been and that I had to try to move on. Hopefully, one day, with somebody new.

A funny thing about this song is the sound effect running through it that sounds a bit like a chicken. It's there because while I was walking through Laurel Canyon, there was a cockerel crowing its morning song, and the sound of it got stuck in my head. So yes, I have a chicken doing backing vocals on this one.

• • •

Apart from the songwriting and my renewed efforts in exercising and healthy eating, there was something else I discovered in my search for some clarity of mind. Ayahuasca. If I'd been at a different point in my life, I mightn't have been open to trying it, but here I was, up for giving it a go!

For those who might not know, ayahuasca is a substance derived from the Banisteriopsis caapi plant, which is native to the Amazon. It has a long history among various indigenous peoples throughout the region, who take it ceremonially as medicine, administered by a shaman. It can be a kind of psychedelic tea but can also be taken in different ways, and it can create altered states of consciousness, taking you on a journey.

While I was out and about one day, I bumped into someone I'd worked with on Broadway, and had since become good friends with. At the time, he was hosting occasional ayahuasca ceremonies in his home and invited me to come along to one.

The idea of the ceremony is to set an intention at the start, to know where you want to go on your journey and what you want to achieve. The aim is to then connect with your emotions surrounding that intention. Sometimes that works, but sometimes you just have to let all that go by the by and simply see what blows through on the wind and what the medicine brings out in you. It's not an exact science.

There are all kinds of different ceremonies: some with twenty or more people who go on a journey for several days, and others, like the one I went to, which are more intimate – six to eight people. They can sometimes even work like a therapy session, with people in the group talking and helping one another work through whatever they need to work through.

On the night of that first ceremony, I was nervous. Of course, I'd done some research, but I really had no idea what to expect. So, when I turned up that night to my friend's beautiful home, I had an open mind along with major butterflies.

As this was my first experience, I decided not to go too heavy. Ultimately, this made for a peaceful experience where I felt fully aware of my surroundings. Along with the ayahuasca, I took a pill of white lily, which is a flowering plant native to the Mediterranean, Middle East and Asia, and is said to help you open your heart and accept peace. And yes, that's where the name of the song came from: 'White Lily Fields', which I wrote with Nick Bradley about the experience.

For me, it wasn't a scary process at all. I was sitting in a room, with low lights and gentle meditative music playing, while calming images were projected onto the ceiling. Yes, I felt a gentle buzz at first, but I was quite happy staying in my lane while others had a more intense experience. That was fine by me.

Eventually, I found myself in this fabulous, alternative state, but still aware of all that was happening around me. Everything seemed clearer and more vivid. I stared at my hand, noticing every single tiny ridge and valley of my fingerprints. It was as if I could see everything I was made of and how I was formed. In my peripheral vision, I saw shadows moving past me. In the midst of my dreamy loveliness, these shadows felt like the spirits of people I'd lost, loved ones who'd come back to guide me through or look after me. It was a weird feeling, yes, but not scary. For me, it was just clarity. It was all very calm and controlled, and I knew reality was still there all around me.

During that first ceremony, I found myself staring at a painting on my host's wall. It was of a woman holding a bunch of coloured balloons in front of her face. In my mind, I saw the balloons start to move, eventually floating away. Behind the balloons, I saw the face of my host's wife. I guess you might call it a hallucination, but it didn't feel like that. In the morning, when I told her what I'd imagined, she looked surprised.

'It's amazing you should say that,' she said.

She then showed me a photograph of herself, wearing the same dress as the woman in the painting, holding a bunch of balloons. The difference was that she was holding up the balloons beside her face rather than in front of it. The painting was of her.

Strangely, what came out of that night for me was the realisation that I needed to release Sarah from my trauma and let her go. It was all very clear; that was what I needed to do. Consequently, the first thing I did when I woke up the next morning was call her.

I thanked Sarah for the love she'd given me over the years, for our children, for understanding and tolerating me as a human being, and I told her that whatever happened, and wherever we both ended up in life, I would always love her and be her friend. So, in an attempt to help myself move on, I realised that, in turn, I had to let her move on. No more drama or stress. I wanted her to be happy and, hopefully, I would be too.

Sometimes, these ayahuasca ceremonies can be quite dramatic and even traumatic – if that's what the medicine brings out. The second time I did it, I went pretty deep, and that wasn't such a happy experience. On my first journey, I'd taken the ayahuasca in chocolate form, but this time I had a slightly larger amount taken in pineapple juice, along with a herbal supplement called sassafras. This time, I had a stronger reaction. I was still very much in control; the difference was, I'd gone into the ceremony not realising the underlying sadness I was feeling at the time, and consequently, that all came out during the evening. I think I'd been pushing it all down, and suddenly, it all came flooding out. It was as if this huge burst of energy flew out of my chest, and suddenly I could breathe freely, letting everything out. Whatever this release was, I felt emotionally drained and incredibly sad at the end of it. While the first ceremony had been about acceptance and letting my old life go, this one was my time to mourn and cry. It hit me hard, and for the next couple of months, I told myself that it wouldn't be an experience I'd be repeating. Why would I do something that made me feel so sad? I've since realised that it had simply helped me to feel how I needed to feel at the time, and now I'd certainly be up for giving it another go.

There are conflicting opinions about the use of ayahuasca and these ceremonies, but there are plenty of studies that highlight the benefits of this kind of medicine, showing how it's helped many people rid themselves or elevate depressive, anxious, and addictive symptoms. Measured and administered correctly, I believe it can be life-altering. For me, it was about fixing rather than getting high. It was stimulation, a challenge, just like swimming under ice would be in the not-too-distant future.

CHAPTER 16

FAMILY

As I write this, I've received some happy news. Grace and Alfie are coming for the Christmas holidays and I get to be a hands-on dad again. They're staying with old school friends in Gloucester for a couple of days, and then coming to stay with me for Christmas. Sarah will also be here for Christmas Day, so I've decided I might even make Christmas dinner; I do love cooking. I suppose my speciality, if I have one, is a traditional Sunday roast. I'm good at those. I also love cooking Italian food, and I make a mean risotto (if I do say so myself!)

I find cooking is good for my head, and I relate the preparation of food to music all the time. To me, the different flavours and fragrances of food are like the different textures and elements of music. Both things also connect to emotions – they make you feel good. Food, like music, can remind you of a place you went to on holiday, a past romance, or your childhood.

One of the new songs I've been working on is called 'Father', which sums up many parts of my childhood in its lyrics. It's a really powerful song for me, even though I didn't write the lyrics myself. Instead, I had been telling the story of my dad and what he meant to me to a wonderful young singer/songwriter I was working with called Leon Stanford. Leon had been sitting, listening to me talking, and it turns out, he was inspired to put what I'd told him into a song. The next day he came into the studio and presented me with this amazing song with beautiful lyrics.

Dad was the most loving, joyful man with such kindness in his green eyes, which he reflected on all of us. Being a manual worker, he had strong hands, and he wore his hair in a quiff that would always fall down over his eyes, so he was constantly brushing it away from his face. All Dad wanted was a peaceful, happy life and the best for his family. He loved his Sunday dinners and a glass of wine, and as far as I was concerned, there was nothing he couldn't do well. If he put up a shelf, you could be certain that the wall it was on would fall before that shelf ever did.

Aside from Dad, I mainly grew up with girls around me, my mum and sisters – Annie, Frances, Maria, Pauline and Theresa. By the time I came along, my brothers – Joe, John and Michael – had pretty much left home. My brother Joe had gone into the fire brigade, and John joined the Royal Air Force when I was still relatively young. I always loved it when John came home because he was like my hero. My other brother, Michael, wasn't around for long either. He went off to study to become a priest but eventually left the seminary. Michael loved opera too, and the first time I heard *La Bohème*, it was Michael who played it to me on a crackly old recording of it sung by Jussi Björling and Victoria de los Ángeles.

Of course, with such a big family, there were always visitors. My sisters had their friends and their boyfriends and their boyfriends' friends over, so the house was often bursting at the seams. Consequently, I did my best to stay out of the way a lot of the time. I'd hide in the garden or at the school fields or the beach.

We used to go hiking as a family, in the Lake District. Just as I used to hide away when the house was buzzing full of people, I used to do something similar while we were walking in the mountains. As my family walked ahead of me, I would see how far I could lag behind them all without anyone noticing and calling out for me to catch up. I don't know why, I just felt like I wanted to put distance between me and everyone else. Sometimes, the gap would get bigger and bigger with no one looking around or checking on me. I remember thinking once, would they ever miss me if they turned around and I wasn't there?

I have no idea why I felt like this (and trust me, I've had extensive therapy sessions over the years where the subject came up). Even now, I still have those moments, wondering, will people remember me when I'm not around? Will anyone care? It's a feeling I've lived with my entire life, and a big part of the struggles I've had with mental health. It was something I had to face, big time, while I was in rehab.

One day, it actually happened. I slowed down my pace as my family trooped across the hills. I fell further and further behind without anyone noticing until eventually I slowed to a stop and watched as the last of them disappeared over a ridge and out of sight.

I was on my own. A six or maybe seven-year-old kid, alone up a mountain in the Lake District. I remember the thrill of it, and the shock of it; looking around and listening to nothing. It was almost silent apart from the wind in the trees and a few birds. I didn't move. I just stood there, calmly waiting and waiting to see how long it would be before someone noticed I wasn't there, and they came searching for me.

I think that experience, and those fears of being forgotten, make being away from my kids so impossible to bear sometimes. I never want them to feel like they've been left behind by me, forgotten or abandoned. And I don't ever want them to purposely distance themselves from me.

I'm happy to report that this is something I have learned to deal with over time. I've realised that whoever we are and whatever difficulties we're going through, people love us and we are all important. We all make an impact in the world, and we all matter. We are all a part of someone's life and we'll be missed if we're not around.

Eventually that day, it was my dad who I saw walking back over the ridge to come and find me. He was always the one who came to the rescue. If I ever needed saving, he was the one who saved me.

Dad was really my first influence, my first teacher when it came to music. His record collection was extensive and covered many different types of music, from big band leaders Glenn Miller and Tommy Dorsey, to American country artists like Slim Whitman and Jim Reeves, to opera. He really was a huge fan of classical music, particularly the great tenors, like Caruso, but his favourite singer was an Austrian called Richard Tauber. One of Tauber's most famous songs, 'You Are My Heart's Delight', or 'Dein ist mein ganzes Herz' in German, an aria from a 1929 operetta called *The Land Of Smiles*, was the first song I ever auditioned with.

Dad had a sense of fun, and he loved to dance. If he heard a rhythm start up on the radio, he'd start tapping his foot and end up bopping. He'd jive around the kitchen, or break into the Charleston. These are some of my fondest and clearest memories of my dad; him picking me up, holding me, and dancing with me. Teaching me to learn to love music.

My musical journey really began when he heard me drumming rhythms on my pillows in my room one day. Back then, I had drumsticks but no drums – there was no way we'd have been able to afford a brand-new drum kit, even though Mum and Dad knew I loved to play. Instead, I'd arrange a bunch of cushions and pillows around me, just like a kit, going from the highest sounding – when they were hit – to the lowest. I'd put my radio on and start drumming along to the songs, getting completely lost in it.

When Dad peeped around the door one day to see what I was up to, I guess he knew that pillows weren't going to cut it for someone who loved playing as much as I did.

One evening, he shouted up from downstairs, sounding a bit cross.

'Alfie, come down here, you're making a racket.' I came down and apologised, but there was more. 'And you've left a load of your stuff in the living room, go and tidy it up.'

'Sorry, Dad,' I said.

When I opened the living room door, there sat a drum kit we'd seen in a second-hand shop a couple of weeks before.

I couldn't believe it, and let's face it, I was lucky. I mean, the last thing most parents want to buy an energetic twelve-year-old lad is a drum kit.

As well as music, I got my love of cars from my dad. He loved his vintage cars, and he would get hold of an old Austin A30 or an old Moggy Minor cheap, and then tinker around with them and fix them up. I loved watching him do all that, and it's why I went on to be a car mechanic, too.

Sometimes, he'd take me out for a drive in one of the classic beauties he'd recently got back on the road. If I close my eyes, I can still see him, sitting there in his parka jacket. I can smell the leather of the seats and feel the walnut of the dashboard under my fingers. I can hear the click of his wedding ring on the hard steering wheel, every time he turned a corner – click, tap, click.

His other hobbies were making his own beer and wine, which he enjoyed, and he also loved his food. Actually, the more I think about it, the more I realise just how many things I did get from my dad.

Dad was a process worker in a chemical factory, and a number of people who worked with him had been affected by the chlorine gas they were working with. If I'm honest, I think that's what did for my dad. Like some of the others, Dad died of a brain tumour at the age of sixty-three.

A couple of months before he died, we all gathered in the living room of our family home, where Dad was now sleeping full-time. That day, as he drifted in and out of sleep, I noticed him looking quite sad – by then, he knew he wasn't going to survive the tumour. He said he wanted to speak to his children one by one, so we turned off the TV, which had been on in the background, and took our turns sitting with him. Dad told us all how much loved us and also bequeathed us some of his possessions, giving me a watch that belonged to his grandfather.

'I know I haven't got long left, but somehow we'll meet again, Son,' he told me, and he seemed sure of it.

On the day my father passed away, I held him, one arm around his shoulder, my other hand in his. When he finally went, I actually felt him leave his body as it relaxed. It was as if he'd climbed out of his body and left the room.

I lived with the thought of his words for quite a while after he died; the idea of somehow seeing my dad again. Would he appear at the side of a stage while I was performing, or would I look down and see him in the front row of an audience at a show? It was a nice image to have. A few months after he passed, I walked into the kitchen of my mum's house to make her a cup of tea. As I was making the tea, putting the leaves from the tea caddy into the pot, then picking up the spoon and stirring it, vigorously rattling the spoon around, I caught sight of my arm and my hand and froze for a second. It was my dad's hand I was looking at, and my dad's arm. I was standing how he stood, moving how he moved. I realised how much like him I was, that I was a part of him, and it made sense now, him telling me that we would see one another again. The truth was, I'd never have to look for him because he'd always be with me.

I suppose that's why, when I was invited to duet with Vera Lynn on the song 'We'll Meet Again' for the *Vera Lynn 100* album in 2017, it meant such a lot to me. Those words always strike a chord in me. Funnily enough, the gold disc I got for that album is the only disc I've ever put up in my house. I've never displayed any of my accolades for tour sales or record sales on the wall, mainly because they've got my face on them, and I don't want to be looking at that every time I walk into a room. Plus, now Michael's face is on a lot of them as well, there's even less reason to want to put them up.

In the first verse of my song 'Father', the lyric talks about him playing a beat into my heart, teaching me rhythm and giving me a voice and a love of music. The chorus lyric talks about him telling me we'd meet again, and the second verse is about him singing songs to me when I was little. 'Baby Mine' from *Dumbo* was one of the songs he sang, also the Elvis song 'Big Boots', and 'Beautiful Dreamer' by Slim Whitman. It also talks of a handle left on the day of his wake, which is a reference to the handle on one side of his coffin, which snapped under the strain of the strap as it was being lowered into the ground, flying out of the coffin and landing at my and my brother's feet. It was a strange, poignant moment, quickly punctuated by a quip that if my dad had put that handle on, it would never have broken off.

There's also a line about climbing on feathers to the sky, which refers to the strange story of my mother talking to a neighbour of ours, a couple of days after Dad's funeral.

'What were all those white feathers flying up in the air in your back garden on the day of Alf's wake, Pat?' he asked my mum.

She just looked at him, thinking he might have lost the plot.

'You know, when you were all throwing white feathers into the air; is that a Catholic thing or something?' he said. 'I could just see this tower of feathers going upward, really high, and then falling back down again.'

'I don't know what you're talking about, Eddie,' Mum said. 'Nobody was throwing any feathers up in the air that day.'

When Mum came home, she was quite pale as she told us what Eddie had said.

It was such a strange thing to hear – and confusing. One of those weird events in life you can't explain. It was such an emotional time; perhaps, on the day of my dad's funeral, there was more going on than we knew.

The final reference is him singing in his 'land of smiles',

which is the opera that his favourite song, 'You Are My Heart's Delight', came from, and the question 'did you walk with my children for miles?' is wondering if he somehow met my children somewhere before they were born and came to us. It always makes me sad to think that he never got to meet them here, in the world.

I think many of us grow up, especially in our teenage years, thinking we will be more than our parents, better, somehow, and that we will know and experience more than they have. In so many ways, though, we're made up of our parents. We all have a little bit of them running through us.

I'd like to think I've given my children strength and perhaps shown them ways to get through some of the problems they might face in life. I'd like them to remember me as being fun and loving and to feel proud of what I've achieved, learning from my successes and my mistakes. Mostly, I'd like to think that through my example, they'll believe in themselves and follow their dreams.

CHAPTER 17

FREEZING MY FEARS

Throughout my career, things have come across my path at the right time. Whether it's been certain roles, characters in operas or musical theatre, TV or recording projects, opportunities always seem to come along just when they're meant to.

This was certainly the case with *Freeze the Fear with Wim Hof* – a TV series where celebrities undertook physically and mentally demanding challenges in sub-zero temperatures. I'd literally only just discovered Wim on YouTube, a couple of weeks before I got the call. I'd been sitting in my apartment in Salt Lake, still navigating the new challenges of single life, scrolling through videos when I came across this long-haired, bearded guy doing all these weird breathing techniques and sitting in barrels of freezing iced water. Of course, I was intrigued. Well, actually, I thought he was crazy, but I kept watching. There was something about his approach to life and his connection to nature that fascinated me.

A week or ten days after discovering Wim, came the call from my management, telling me about his upcoming TV project. The producers were looking for celebrities to take part in something that was going much deeper than the usual reality television show. They were interested in people who'd struggled or had been through some kind of trauma and were up for facing those things head-on, through a series of challenges in, on and under ice. After sitting down with the show's producers and talking it through, I immediately knew this was something I wanted to do. In fact, I went into it without thinking of it as a TV show at all. I went intending to heal myself. It didn't really matter whether or not there was a film crew capturing our every move; I'd have done it without the cameras.

In many ways, this approach was liberating. I had no thoughts of trying to put the right personality across or being a certain way in front of the cameras. It was simply about a healing process and what I could achieve for myself. I saw the experience as something that could help me change and hopefully move on, which is why I say it came along at just the right time. A crucially important time, in fact.

I'd heard people talk of rebirth. You often do, don't you? The idea of somehow leaving the old you behind, of starting again with a clean page. Fresh and new. I don't think I'd ever really thought about what it meant before or how it might come about.

The truth is, being reborn isn't something that just happens in a moment of blinding revelation, at least that's not how I see it. It's something you have to make happen, or at least allow to happen. It's a choice you make for yourself.

During the filming of the show, I'd made that choice. It was a conscious decision to leave the terrible pain I'd been suffering behind me. Or rather, below me. Under the ice.

We were in the Italian Alps for almost a month. January 2022. Because of continuing Covid rules in Italy, we all had to isolate for ten days, and during that time Wim tested positive for Covid, which held up the start of filming even further.

As far as living conditions went for the duration of the show, there really was no challenge. We definitely weren't slumming it; it was like the highest end of glamping you can possibly imagine. We had great food, we were warm – there was a gorgeous log-burning fire that I spent a lot of time sitting down next to – and the beds were nice and cosy. They did everything to make our environment comfortable. It was peaceful too, probably because we weren't allowed any phones, iPads or computers – just like in rehab, they got handed in before filming began. I suppose that was one of the hardest things for me: not being able to talk to my kids for a month. Having already been separated from them so much, that felt very tough. Not just for me, but for everyone who couldn't talk to their loved ones throughout the duration of the show. The no-tech rule was there to give us all a chance to bond and communicate with one another without distraction, to embrace the environment we were in and to really think about the things we were there to address. Everyone there had something they needed to work on, and we needed to fully engage with the process. So, there we all were living in this strange world without the intrusion of social media or the knowledge of what was going on in the world, which is a very rare thing to experience and not always easy. In fact, towards the end of filming, when we were all tired and wanting to get back to reality, being cut off from family was probably the thing that had taken its toll the most.

As far as the sub-zero temperatures went, well, I suppose coming from the north of England, I'm no stranger to a bit of cold weather. Plus, I've done a bit of freshwater swimming up north. That said, standing on a frozen lake in front of a hole that's been chainsawed out of the ice is something else entirely. I remember my first go at it, before our very first plunge into the water, standing on the edge, colder than I'd ever been in my life. Staring down into a circle of black water and wondering what the hell I'd let myself in for. They'd even shovelled some snow in to make it look even colder, so I had no idea what to expect.

You'd think I'd have been a bit more apprehensive, watching the people who went before me, but I was actually quite excited. We'd been hanging around for some time by then, waiting to start the challenges, and this was the first cold water one. I was eager and ready to embrace it. When it was time for me to go, I took off my jacket and took a breath to prepare. I was literally taking a leap of faith, that's how it felt. I crossed my arms over my chest and jumped. I suppose I'd thought about what it might feel like, plunging into that freezing water, but nothing could have prepared me for the effect on my body. Oh my goodness, it took my breath away. When your body hits that shock of cold, it tenses up, and your instinct is to clench every part of yourself in an attempt to be warm. That is the worst thing you can do. As I surfaced from the water, gasping for breath, Wim was on the ice in front of me, shouting enthusiastically in his Dutch accent.

'Keep breathing, deep breath, just keep breathing.'

My mind was all over the place, but I tried to focus on Wim's voice and all the breathing techniques we'd learned so far.

So I listened. I kept breathing until, eventually, my body started to relax. Then I thought, *Hang on, this is really cool. It actually feels good.* I ended up hanging out in that icy hole while hosts Holly Willoughby and Lee Mack interviewed me. I just felt so relaxed. And that eerie black water seemed to get brighter; when I visualise it now, it had turned blue and clear. It felt very natural for me, being in that water and in those elements, surrounded by the Alps. It was beautiful, and I think I could have stayed there for much longer. I wanted to stay in longer; it felt good. In the end, Wim had to tell me to get out. Little did I realise that the real challenge is getting *out* and having the cold hit you. Now, that was really hard.

Still, I wasn't the only one taking a leap of faith. The idea of being submerged in ice was completely alien to footballer Patrice Evra, and weather reporter Owain Wyn Evans was absolutely terrified before that first challenge. Like me, he got very emotional.

I found it very hard watching my fellow campmates struggling with what they were going through. I get emotional when I see other people upset. I always have. I think it's because when I see unhappiness in someone, I want to fix it. I want to make things better and help to make them feel better. In fact, one of the hardest things for me is seeing someone upset when I may have been the cause of it. That's heartbreaking.

There was also a joy in seeing people work through their trauma and get better. I can't speak for everyone, but it seemed like we all came out with a more positive outlook.

Despite being together almost the entire time, all the campmates got on well. When we were doing the challenges, one after the other, there was bound to be a natural competitive element, but stronger than that was the sense that we all wanted to see our fellow campmates succeed and do well. The competition was more with ourselves than with other people. The challenge was facing our own fears and emotions, rather than being better than the person who went before you.

I became friends with Owain Wyn and, also *Strictly Come Dancing* professional Dianne Buswell – we became quite close. I also got on very well with Gabby Logan and Tamzin Outhwaite. In fact, it was just a very nice group of people, and I still care for them and dearly hope they're all doing well and moving forward with their lives, as I'm trying to. In many ways, though, I was just on my own journey, as I'm sure others were. I honestly didn't sign up simply to make a TV show, although that is, of course, what we were doing. For me, it was about challenging myself, letting go of the past and coming back a better person.

Of course, a lot of the things we did on the show were more for the television show than anything else. Just for the visuals. Doing a yoga pose at the end of a plank above a ravine, for instance. I'm not sure what that did for me mentally, but it was a nice thing to have done anyway. Charging down the face of a mountain was also a blast, although when I was halfway down, presenter Lee Mack decided to make things even more challenging.

'Hey Alfie, give us a song,' he shouted down the cliff at me.

'I've just legged it face first down a mountain,' I shouted back.

'I don't care,' came the reply.

OK, I thought, *we're filming, so I'll give it a shot.* I gave them all a quick blast of the climax of 'Nessun Dorma,' to cheers and whoops from my fellow contestants, still at the top of the cliff. It wasn't the greatest performance I'd ever given, but it was a fair effort, given I was practically dangling hundreds of feet above the ground.

'That was fun,' I told Lee afterwards, 'but it's not easy singing when you're being choked by a harness.'

It was the ice challenges that were the real test for me. That's why, when we were asked to take part in what was one of the toughest challenges of the series, swimming under several inches of ice for six metres, I decided I was taking it all down with me:

the mistakes I'd made, the pain I felt, the trauma and the sense of loss that had enveloped my whole existence. It was all going with me, deep into that black water below, but I was coming up without it. It was the only way I was ever going to be able to move forward.

This wasn't exactly a spur-of-the-moment thing either. As soon as I heard about that particular challenge, my intention was to emerge on the other side of it a clearer, stronger man with the opportunity of a new beginning, of starting again.

Before the challenge, we listened to the build-up from Holly, Lee and Wim, telling us how dangerous it was and how focused we needed to be. Wim also told us that down there, looking upward, the sun coming through the ice looked like diamonds. I remember wondering if I'd have time to appreciate any of that while fighting to pull myself through freezing water and up through a little hole. I doubted it very much.

While all this was going on, the skies opened, and it started to snow. I couldn't believe that at the moment when we were about to throw ourselves in a hole cut in the snow and swim below thick ice, the gods had thrown that on us as well.

I was ready for it, though. I'd known this challenge was coming, I'd known it was on the cards. I'd built it up in my mind, not as something to be terrified of, but as something that would allow me to shed all the things I no longer needed: the pain, the past, the mistakes – all of it! I'd visualised myself doing it and completing it.

It's amazing how much strength there is in visualisation.

I spend a lot of time thinking about how an upcoming show or appearance might go. In the run-up to an important event, I'll picture myself actually doing the performance, imagining myself on stage in front of the audience. I see the room, the faces of the people, what I'm wearing, who I'm looking at. I feel the environment and the heat from the lights. I even hear the musicians. Then, when it comes to the actual show, it's nowhere near as scary because I feel like I've already lived it all before.

Still, standing on stage and singing was something I'd done a fair few times, whereas this . . . well, this was something else entirely.

After my under-ice swim, the final challenge was the bridge swing, and it was more terrifying than anything else we'd done. Leaping backwards off a terrifyingly high bridge with a line attached around our waist. This was, without doubt, the biggest challenge for me. In the run-up to it I once again visualised what I thought it would be like, the sensation of falling, of letting go, of falling backwards and swinging under and through a bridge, hundreds of feet off the ground. On the morning of it, I felt so stressed, I couldn't settle down. Part of me wanted to make a run for it, while another part of me couldn't wait to get it over and done with. One thing was for sure: I had to do it. This was the pinnacle of the show, and we'd all seen the bridge we were going to fall from.

Once again, I told myself this was all about starting again; that when I swung through the bridge, I was swinging into a new world. A new existence and a new beginning. Writing it all down now, I suppose it all sounds very dramatic. But when you're doing something as incredible and life-enhancing as we were on that trip, cut off from the rest of the world for the best part of a month, that's exactly how it feels.

I was scared. It's funny, until that moment, up there on the bridge, I never really thought of myself as being afraid of heights, but there it was. I was terrified and I said so! It wasn't like I imagined a bungee jump would be, where you're attached by your feet, and you can see the line and what's going to catch you as you fall. This line was attached around my waist and went below me and underneath the bridge, so I actually couldn't see the thing that was going to stop me from plummeting into the abyss. OK, so my common-sense head told me it was there because I'd been attached to it before-hand, but not being able to see it was the overriding thought at that moment. As far as I was concerned, I was basically going to be free-falling.

As I stood up there, waiting to fall, I wondered if the fact that I'd left so much pain and trauma behind me under the ice had given me a new lease of life and purpose. Had I suddenly felt more positive about the future and about life, only to find myself risking it by throwing myself off a bridge? Was that why I was so scared?

'Breathe out the past; breathe in the future,' Wim called out.

In the past, when I'd been through a really tough period or things had gone badly in my life, I'd often asked myself, can things possibly get any worse? That notion had often instilled a recklessness in me. It made me brave, or maybe stupid – I'm not sure which. Probably a bit of both. I'd do things quite blindly and without much thought for the consequences. I think when you release that trauma of the past, you get more of a sense of the future, and you begin to care about what's coming. The opportunities of life and the idea of moving on and surviving become more precious. I think this was what was happening to me, up there on that bridge.

'Tell me when you're ready to go,' Wim said.

Looking down from a three-inch-wide ledge, I took in the space below me, the fall, as so many emotions flooded through me: scared, excited, distraught, sad … but mostly scared. Then the voice in my head – my own voice – telling me how much I'd screwed things up.

What you don't see on the show is me talking to Wim in the moments before the fall. 'I've let so many people down in my life,' I said. 'I've made so many mistakes.'

'That's all in the past,' Wim said. 'You're falling into the future; you're swinging into the future. You have to let all that go.'

He was right. We all make mistakes throughout our lives, but the forward journey has to be about trying to better ourselves day by day.

Now I was ready. I nodded and heard Wim counting down five seconds.

'Five, four, three …'

It felt like the longest five seconds of my life, and as it was happening, all I could think was, *How can I stop this? How can I make it stop?* Answer? I couldn't.

'...two...'

David, the safety guy, was attached to me with a harness which, with the flick of a lever, came off and released me.

'One...'

I hopped backwards and just...fell. I was falling, flying. The force of being dragged towards the ground by gravity from that high up is incredible. Like nothing I could have ever imagined. Terrifying, exhilarating. Falling fast, clenching every sinew of my body tight, waiting for the moment when the line would tighten. When it did, my flight path changed. Now I was swinging underneath the bridge. I sobbed first, so overcome, and then I cried out. It was so freeing. Swinging backwards and forwards under a bridge, hundreds of feet above the ground. It was the freest I'd ever felt. I screamed. I screamed my lungs out. So much so, I lost my voice that day.

I was happy. I was overjoyed. I'd achieved something special.

When I came onto the other side of the bridge, I was so excited, so grateful that I forgot to hug Wim first and grabbed David, the safety guy, hugging him. Then I hugged Wim. Then I hugged everyone.

The overriding feeling from doing all these challenges was that I had, in many ways, taken back control. For so long, I'd felt like a pinball in a machine, being flipped and thrown around, just going wherever the next hit took me. Fate had its way, and I had no say. After doing these challenges and that show, I no longer feel that way. I know I can't control everything that happens in life, none of us can. What I can control, the thing I do have a say in, is how I deal with and handle what happens. How I act and react to events and situations.

•   •   •

It's been over a year since I recorded the show, and I will admit that on some days I wonder if I'm feeling any better. It's inevitable, I suppose. Our lives are so up and down, and our moods mirror those dips and bumps. Some people are masters of putting their worries to one side and getting on with life. I'm not so good at that. If something is niggling away at me, my whole world can turn sour and I start to struggle. It's during those times that I really do have to push myself to do all those things that I know will make me feel better. Getting outside, exercising, eating well, writing music, singing – they're my tools. That's the key to mental health for me; it's not something we can solve with one cure. It's a continuous journey, and we all need the right tools to help us along.

CHAPTER 18

VEGAS

Las Vegas! Just saying the name of that city in the desert instantly conjures up so many images, doesn't it? I suppose when most people think of Vegas they visualise the strip, the place to go if you want to gamble and let loose. I must admit, I've never really been into gambling. I've probably lost a grand total of about $25 on the tables over the years – hardly a high-roller! But what I do enjoy are the restaurants, cocktail bars and, of course, the shows.

The list of the great artists who've had a residency in Vegas over the years makes your head spin, and I never in my wildest dreams imagined I'd be one of them.

When my manager, Craig Logan, called and told me I'd been offered the chance to play in Vegas – my own residency – I was ecstatic!

'It's at the Westgate Casino,' Craig went on. 'The one where Elvis had his residency.'

'Are you serious?'

He was! Craig had a good relationship with the Westgate, and that's how the whole thing had come about. I think that's what excited me most: the idea of playing that particular venue with its wonderfully rich history. Originally, it was called the International Hotel, opened in 1969, and was the tallest building in the state. The first performer to play there was none other than Barbra Streisand but, for me, the place was special because it was where Elvis Presley took up residence for seven years of sold-out shows. The place is dripping in show business history and I was thrilled to have the opportunity to play there.

At that moment, all sorts of thoughts ran through my head. Me singing in Las Vegas, when I might not have even been a singer if it hadn't been for a fateful moment in a village hall. That's something else I have my dear mum to thank for.

Back when I was a drummer in the school band, we were invited to play at a village hall somewhere in the locale, for a musical celebration of some sort. I can't really remember what the event was, just being there. I must have been about fourteen at the time and probably excited at the prospect of an audience – any audience.

We'd been asked to play a few rock and blues numbers, and, as I'm sure you can imagine, I was as enthusiastic a drummer back then as I am a singer now. Once we got going, I was knocking these tunes out with all the teenage energy I could muster, much to the dismay of the assembled crowd, who clearly weren't as young or enthusiastic about our music as we were. You could see it on their faces; they basically hated us.

'They're terrible,' somebody squawked in between numbers.

'It's ridiculously loud,' somebody else piped up. 'Awful noise.'

We actually weren't terrible at all. The young guys I was playing with at the time were, and still are, amazing guitarists. That said, we were going for it, hammer and tongs, and the sound system, whatever it was, probably wasn't too clever or too easy on the ears. It got to the point during our enthusiastically banging repertoire where people were actually covering their ears and shouting out for us to shut up or turn it down.

Suddenly, in the midst of it all, my mum stepped forward. 'Alf, why don't you sing a song?' she said.

'Really?'

'Yes, go on, sing something. Let them hear your voice.'

I stood up from the drums and headed towards the microphone, which is when someone shouted out, 'Please no, he's not going to sing as well, is he?'

'That's the last thing we need, him singing,' another cry went up.

I looked over at Mum, nodding her encouragement, then put my head down and strode across to the mic.

I sang 'Somewhere' from *West Side Story*, completely a cappella, and after a couple of bars, the whole atmosphere had lifted. I was no longer the noisy, annoying drummer in a school band. I was a fourteen-year-old boy on stage, singing a classic song in a way none of them would have ever expected. The mood of the entire audience had changed, and by the time I finished singing, they were on their feet, applauding.

Afterwards, I jumped off the stage and headed over to my mum, but I'd only walked a few steps before I was surrounded by a crowd of local women and families.

'What on earth are you doing playing drums? You're a singer,' someone said.

'You've got an amazing voice, why are you hiding at the back of the stage?'

The sentiment was echoed by everyone who approached me. I remember asking myself, *Are they right? Am I really wasting my time playing the drums?*

It was a moment that cemented something inside me. This was something I hadn't considered. Sure, I knew I loved singing and could carry a tune, but I had no idea I might have the power to have that effect on people; that I could do that to a room, to an audience. I've always believed in the power that music has or can have in people's lives; that was probably one of the first times I'd seen that power in action, and it was all thanks to Mum.

She was on my mind so much during my Vegas shows. It should have been the time of my life, but with her being so ill, it was, at times, challenging and hard for me to let loose and enjoy. Despite knowing she was in really good hands, she was in the back of my mind the whole time.

I had to push through, though. I was determined to throw myself into those shows and give them everything I had. This was a fantastic opportunity for me, and I wanted to make it work.

I was gung-ho and excited to get the show up and running by the time I arrived in Vegas. I wanted to show the Vegas audiences the best of me, all sides of me, so I'd put together a specific show, something that didn't pull any punches. My aim was to perform songs that everyone knew, and, with a few exceptions, keep the mood lively and up tempo. It was important to me that everyone was on their feet, dancing – that's what I wanted from this show. Everyone's world had been smaller and unhappier for the past couple of years, and my set was designed to lift them. Also, like any Vegas entertainer, I was expected to put people in a good mood before they head off to the tables and fritter away some money. That's what keeps the casinos happy!

Tickets for the show had sold fairly well; in fact, quite a lot of my UK fans were coming over to see it. What I think helped even more was my appearance on an early morning news show. I dragged myself out of bed at an ungodly hour to get to the studio, and during the interview, as I sat there still jet-lagged and slightly spaced out, the show's host smiled and asked, 'Would you sing us a little bit of "Nessun Dorma", Alfie?'

I thought, *It's six o'clock in the morning, and you want to hear Puccini with a B flat top note?* Of course, I did it, and actually I'm glad I did. After that, ticket sales for my Vegas show started to go crazy. Rather appropriately, the title of 'Nessun Dorma' in English is 'Let No One Sleep'.

Leading up to the show, I couldn't stop thinking about how the place was steeped in entertainment history, and you get a real sense of that while you're in the building. Stars like Wayne Newton, Barry Manilow and Liberace have performed there, among so many others. But it was Elvis that was always on my mind!

Waiting to go on that first night, I was nervous, but as always, I'd gone through the process of using visualisation, imagining myself doing the show, despite my head being all over the place at times because of Mum.

Now I was sitting in the very same dressing room that Elvis had before his first show in July 1969. I remembered the footage I'd seen of him being escorted from his room back-stage to the theatre, through all the staff quarters and towards the stage. Now here I was, walking that same route. Walking in Presley's footsteps.

Beneath the stage, I walked down the hallway, then took the same elevator Elvis would have taken as he headed to the packed showroom. When the elevator door opened, I walked towards the stage, stopping at the spot by a column where he would always stop before touching the wall and saying a prayer. Looking down at my feet, I noticed the small square patch of floor where he'd stood each night. It's aged and worn and still coated with the old varnish. These are the actual floorboards Elvis stood on before he walked out to perform his 636 sold-out performances, untouched by any of the renovations over the years.

I was still for a minute or so, listening to the buzz of the crowd, taking it all in, and then it was time.

The start of the show is a bit of fun. It begins on screen with a little cartoon Alfie waking up in London, getting dressed, travelling through the sights of London in a taxi to the airport, and then getting off the plane in Vegas. It ends with cartoon me running into the Westgate Casino and onto the stage, which is where the real me takes over. Then it's straight into a fiery, no-nonsense, set: Journey's 'Don't Stop Believin', a Frankie Valli medley, some Neil Diamond, a bit of Elton and a big Elvis medley at the end. I throw a bit of classical in there too – a couple of Neapolitan songs and an operatic aria. And, of course, 'Bring Him Home'. I'm not sure I'd have been able to leave the building without doing that one.

The audiences in Vegas are lively and vibrant; everybody is out to have a great time. That's what I loved most about it. The minute you step out on the stage, they're with you. It was wonderful, and I wish Mum could have been there to see it.

· · ·

The idea for the *Together in Vegas* album with Michael came about because of my residency there. We thought it would be a great idea to celebrate some of the great artists who've played in the great rooms of Vegas and to celebrate the city, and we wanted to make the whole thing fiery and upbeat. At one point, we did look at recording some slow, more emotive numbers – something by Celine Dion for example – but we just couldn't find a Celine song that sat with the spirit of the album or that screamed Las Vegas. We wanted to uplift and give people energy during difficult times, rather than performing big ballads.

Alongside the record came the opportunity to record an accompanying TV special, utilising all the things that Vegas is known for. We performed songs from the album in various locations: 'The Gambler' at a saloon in the Venetian, and 'Luck Be a Lady' at the city's famous Neon Museum. And while I took a helicopter ride, Michael got to peruse Liberace's famously outrageous wardrobe. We visited the wedding chapel where stars like Elvis, Britney Spears, Sinatra and Joan Collins have all been married at one time or another. We even sang at the wedding of a British couple (the bride was a big Ball and Boe fan) who'd gone over to Vegas to tie the knot.

While we were there filming, I was invited to the ex-governor's house to sing. It was a lovely event, where I pulled out the big guns, singing 'Bring Him Home' for the assembled guests. Later on that same trip, the Westgate Casino invited me back to sing at an event in the Elvis Presley Suite, which, back in the day, was pretty much the entire top floor of the casino and where Elvis lived during his residency. It's since been remodelled into three separate suites.

The Elvis Presley Suite is ostentatious and over the top: an Italian design with marble floors, grand chandeliers, pillars, paintings and vaulted ceilings galore. There's baroque gold trim and frescos as far as the eye can see, statutes of horses and classical figures, plush rugs and a grand piano thrown in for good measure. I guess my tastes are slightly more restrained, but it looks like somewhere eighteenth-century French or Italian royalty might live.

When I walked into the suite that day with Gordy, the casino's PR manager, my jaw dropped. It was full of the most gorgeous women in beautiful dresses, wearing sashes.

'Gordy, what is this event I'm singing at, exactly?'

'Oh, this is the Miss America party,' he said.

'Right,' I said. 'Why not?'

It was another one of those moments, I suppose. Something that if I'd been told I'd be doing as a boy – singing to Miss America contestants in the Elvis Suite of a Las Vegas hotel, surrounded more by glitz, gold and marble than I knew existed – I wouldn't have believed it in a million years.

CHAPTER 19

BACK IN THE UK

I was in the middle of rehearsing with a band in Los Angeles, getting ready for the warm-up show for my first Las Vegas residency when one morning, I got a call from my sister. She had bad news.

'Mum's been rushed to the hospital; she's had a pretty serious stroke.'

It was in May 2022 and I decided that, for my mum, I had to make the move back to the UK – so a pre-Vegas warm-up concert in Utah was completely out of the question.

The hardest part about going back was that I'd literally be leaving my kids behind in another country. On one hand, I tried to be optimistic, thinking about building a new existence for myself in London. On the flip side, I was tortured by thoughts of being so far away from Grace and Alfie, who are now fifteen and eleven. How on earth was I going to make that part of my life work? It's one thing being in another house or even another town, but now my kids would be on another continent. If I thought I could have earned enough to support us all working in America, I'd probably have stayed, but the UK was where my work was. I needed to be there. Post-Vegas I had some more shows to do in the UK, and Michael and I were recording 'Together in Vegas', which was due to be released towards the end of that year.

The news about my mum was a shock, but she had been declining for a while. We'd been told by doctors that she had dementia a year or so before, and we could all see the early stages of it. Then, when I called her one day, she answered the phone sounding a bit odd. Well enough, but there was something not quite right.

'How are you doing, Mum?' I asked.

'Yes, I'm doing OK, thank you,' she said.

There was definitely something strange about the way she sounded, but I couldn't put my finger on what it was.

'What have you been up to?' I asked.

'Well, I cleaned out the fireplace and swept the yard. And I've done a bit of work around the house,' she said. 'Who am I talking to?'

I was completely thrown. 'It's me, Mum. Alf, your son.'

'Alf? Oh, right,' she said. 'Well, it's nice to meet you anyway.'

My heart sank like a stone. 'OK, Mum, well, I'm going to have to go now.'

I hung up the phone and burst into tears. It was like this wasn't Mum anymore; like she'd gone. I know there are so many people who will have gone through this with elderly relatives; it's so very hard to get your head around.

It's heartbreaking watching your parents grow old, especially when they were once so strong and sturdy. It's also hard getting used to the idea that Mum might not be around for too much longer. It's brought up a lot of things for me and stirred a lot of memories.

Mum had been through tough times, especially as a kid. She lost her mother when she was twelve and had a stepmother who she didn't get along with and didn't treat her particularly well. To add to her troubles, Mum got TB, ending up in a sanatorium where she spent a year getting better. The sanitorium was run by nuns, and at one point, Mum was thinking of becoming a nun herself. She was a postulant in a convent near Southampton, where she cooked, cleaned and learned how to knit and make clothes. Now that really would have changed the course of history, her being a nun. No Alfie for a start!

When she was twenty-one, though, she travelled back to Fleetwood to visit her father, who by then was very ill. It was then she met Alf, my dad, and they fell in love. Well, not quite straight away. He was an errand boy for the Co-op at the time, cycling around Fleetwood delivering groceries. When he spotted my mum walking along the street, he was so dazzled by her, he hit a lamppost and came off his bike, sending his stash of fruit and veg all over the road. Apparently, Mum didn't even notice him, splayed out across the pavement, and trotted off down the road. Dad was determined, though. He persevered, and after a short courtship, they married in March 1954.

As the youngest of four boys and five girls, Mum went from almost becoming a nun to having nine kids. That's quite a U-turn.

I wrote a song about that first meeting between Mum and Dad called 'Quicksteppin'' – the quickstep being one of Dad's favourite dances. It talks about him flying head over the handlebars and into her arms.

As a mother, she was a strong lady because she had to be; a fiery, loving woman who worked really hard. I can't even imagine how she did what she did, bringing up nine children. She was a fantastic cook, who loved to laugh and sing songs, although she's always been a terrible singer. My particular talent definitely came from someone other than Mum, who's one of those people that can start a song in one key and end up in a completely different one. She could be tough, though. She had a strong Catholic faith, which she instilled in us kids, even when we didn't want to hear of it. Church on Sunday, confession, benediction – we went through all of it – and of course, there was plenty of good old-fashioned Catholic guilt. It was hard to take at the time, and I was a bit wayward, I suppose, but I see now that she was simply trying to instil morals in all of us, teaching us to grow up to be good people.

When we lost my dad, it was her I felt for more than myself. At the time, I felt like I was quite prepared for his death. We all were to an extent. Although his illness was quite short, we knew it was coming and that there was nothing to be done about it. In fact, it was much further down the line that I felt his loss and really started to grieve.

Mum, on the other hand, lost the love of her life that day, someone who she spent almost fifty years with. She never met anyone else or even tried to, and now she's been without him for over twenty-five years.

I think when my mum passes away, my comfort will be in knowing they'll be together again.

With the news of Mum's stroke, I knew I needed to get back to the UK as soon as possible. I cancelled the Utah show and headed back to England to be with Mum.

In the end, she was hospitalised for quite a while, but thankfully, she was stable and doing OK, which meant I was still able to go out to Vegas to do my show. It wasn't easy, though. I'd spent time with her and I'd seen she was in good hands and doing well, but you never know what the outcome of something like that might be. As soon as it was over, I was back on a flight to the UK.

Thankfully, Mum is still trucking on, although she didn't come out of the stroke so well. Her speech isn't great, and she's certainly not the same person she was. It's hard to see. When I think about the powerful, vibrant Irish woman I grew up with and have always known, seeing her so vulnerable, unable to look after herself anymore, is heartbreaking.

At the moment, she's living in a nursing home and being very well looked after.

Once I was properly back in the UK, I wanted to throw

myself into work. I felt I needed to rebuild what I'd lost in the two years of Covid. I think it was the same for many people in the live entertainment world. The thing that makes them tick, that they know how to do best – entertain people – had become almost impossible. At the time, it was difficult to even plan for the future, because we just didn't know when or if theatres and venues were going to open up again. Consequently, when things slowly started to open up, everyone moved forward with a great deal of caution and uncertainty.

For the first few months of being back, I lived in a hotel because I had no London home. At some point, I knew I'd have to buy a place, so I'd have a base. My intention was to build my own world back in the UK, a new world, so the kids felt like they had a real home here as well as their home in America. In the meantime, I signed up to an estate agent and rented an apartment. Nothing fancy, just somewhere to live. Somewhere to call home, at least for a while.

I had to start all over again, I knew that, but this time with a new intention, a new mindset. By then, I'd realised how much I often let the things I thought I needed – work, success, recognition – blind me to what really mattered. Nurturing a connection with someone, having someone to love and grow with. In the end, success and fame were secondary, and they certainly didn't always equal happiness. Sometimes, we need reminding of how life should really work. We might have to go through a few dark tunnels to truly realise where the light is and that what's important might be on the other side. I did.

It's a work in progress; I'm a work in progress.

Friends have asked me, 'Are you better now, Alfie?'

What I really want to say is, 'I don't know, are you better?'

We all have some stuff that is hard to cope with in our lives. Many people with the facade of the most wonderful and perfect existence turn out to be hiding pain or unhappiness. I know; I was one of them.

I'm definitely in a better place than I was, yes, but I'm by no means fixed. It's still a day-to-day process that I'm feeling my way through. The difference now is that I have tools in my box to deal with the rough patches. I play my guitar, I phone a friend, I connect with my kids, listen to music or do some exercise. I try to find ways to lift myself up and combat anxiety or depression if I can.

Sometimes, though, we need to connect to the sadness we feel; to accept that's how we're feeling and just sit with it. I do that too sometimes. I acknowledge that I'm feeling low, then accept it's happening and that it will pass. If I'm lucky, it will pass quickly and I'll be able to get on with the rest of my day.

Music is a great help with that. Sometimes, I'll walk around the streets of London with my earphones in, listening to songs that envelop me in the past. Sense memory – recalling the physical sensations and feelings that accompanied an event from your past – can be so useful and important. Going through the process of stimulating sad memories and remembering how they felt helps me work through the sadness. It's the same with playing songs or music that remind you of someone you've lost for whatever reason. Yes, it makes us feel sad, but at the same time, we're giving ourselves permission to feel. That, to me, is important. Music is a powerful thing and it's got me through some really tough times. I'm lucky enough to be able to sing and create music, but it's accessible to everyone. Whether you're sitting in sand dunes, singing your head off with your AirPods in, or dancing around your house in your own private kitchen disco, we can all use the power of music to tap into our positive or negative emotions, our sadness, our happiness, our heartbreak or loss. Using music to deal with things is self-help. It's taking care of yourself in the same way physical exercise is.

CHAPTER 20

NOW

Living in the UK, I FaceTime with my kids every single day, sometimes more than once. We have computer game sessions on our phones and send one another clips and messages. It's not the same as being able to pick them up from school in the evening, but it's beautiful. I love being able to share what I've been doing with them and listening to the stories of their days.

I have a song called 'Stormy Waters' which is a powerful one for me. I was staying in the romantic town of Guildford when it came to me, not long after my Atlantic-wide separation from the family. It was in the middle of the night, and I was suddenly wide awake with all these lyrics flying around my head. I wrote some of them down, then went back to sleep. A while later, I was awake again, scribbling down more words, thoughts and lines. By the time I got up the next morning, I had quite the collection of lyrics, and I took them all into the studio that day.

At the time, before I did *Freeze the Fear*, I'd been going through a period where I'd wake myself up crying every day. I was also speaking to Sarah and the children on the phone each morning – well, it was morning for them, but usually about seven hours after I woke up. The song, then, talks about crying myself awake with visions of my mistakes and of the family being so far away.

Every day at around the same time, the phone would ring, and I'd see Sarah's name light up the screen. I'd be over the moon that I was hearing from my kids, but always nervous, not knowing how Sarah might be with me. Would she be angry? Would she be happy? So, when I sing about the lights turning on in my heart but fear hitting hard, that's the idea behind the line.

The weirdest part is, I could never breathe easy until I'd spoken to them each day, and I knew they were OK. My day literally couldn't start until I'd had that contact. Consequently, I spent much of my time feeling anxious, then once they'd called, I could go about my day.

The idea of sailing through stormy waters is a reference to my children. Sarah had moved on by then, I suppose, but this was a message to them that whatever happened, we'd get through it, and I'd still always be there for them.

I suppose, in the end, this is a song full of hope. It's about moving forward and being happy again.

You can imagine how much spending Christmas with

my kids meant to me. With me being in the UK and them being so far away, every moment was precious. Sarah spent Christmas Eve and Christmas Day with us in the end, but I think she found it harder than I did. It's funny, it felt very natural to me and, I think, for the kids. I suppose I was content to feel like I was in a normal family situation again. The decorations were up, we had presents, and everything looked nice and Christmassy.

I was happy, but having them here brought home to me all that I was missing. This is a very special family, and I miss not being in it all the time. Leaving Sarah was tough, but leaving the kids was even tougher.

Alfie stayed at my place the whole time they were in the UK, and I loved having him with me. He's into computers and games, but he also likes art. He's gentle and has a kind heart and an amazing, infectious spirit.

'Energy' is one of the very positive songs I've written lately, and I wrote it about Alfie. It starts like a lullaby but builds, and on first hearing, the listener might think I'm singing about a love interest or a partner – especially with phrases like, 'when you hold me'. But it's the vision of my son holding me I'm trying to convey.

It's funny; I guess we usually think of a parent as the one doing the holding or comforting when it comes to a child, but my son often comes over to me and pulls me close so that I'm resting my head on his chest. It's something he's always done. He's an amazing, loving kid who knows how to make a person feel nurtured, safe and cared for.

The lyrics of 'Energy' talk about his love of life, his care-free attitude and how I long to be like him and feel like that again. In that sense, I think we have a lot to learn with our children.

Grace is a fantastic young woman who has so much spirit. I clearly remember the day she was born and the deep frown on her face when I first held her in my arms. It was a frown that said, *So you're my dad?* It was as if she knew it all from day one. She often still looks at me with that same frown now. She always seems to have the measure of a person.

She was strong-willed, even as a little girl. I have a vision of her in her bouncy chair attached to the ceiling of our living room. I was introducing her to the joys of Van Halen's 'Jump', and she was bouncing up and down and spinning like crazy. The speed she went was outrageous. To be honest, I'm not sure she's ever really slowed down.

These days, she's into her make-up, clothes and shopping at Brandy Melville, which is an interesting experience for a dad, I can tell you. In case you don't know, it's a trendsetting fashion store where teenagers and young women love to shop. Everything is, bizarrely, one size, and there's not much in the way of bright colours going on. I took her to one of the stores over the Christmas holidays and while we were there, I lost her. The trouble was, nearly every fourteen- or fifteen-year-old girl there looked the same. They all had long, straight, flattened hairstyles, short midriff puffer-jackets, baggy cargo trousers and trainers. I tapped two or three girls on the shoulder before I actually found Grace. It was a nightmare.

Right now, I'm throwing myself into work, so my social life sort of takes a bit of a back seat. After a show, I'll usually come off stage, freshen up, and then if there's an after-show mingle, I'm usually guided around by my management and my team, saying hello and meeting anyone I need to meet. After that, I'll go back to my dressing room and pack my bag. There's usually someone outside your door waiting to escort you to your car, who'll then drive you back to your hotel or on to the next town for the following night's show. Don't get me wrong, it's not a bad existence, but it's certainly a lot less crazy these days.

Having been in a relationship for so long, the thought of meeting new people can be quite daunting. The idea of going on a date is a million miles away from where I want to be or from what I had before. I still crave a home and day-to-day family life. The idea of sharing your life with someone.

Eventually, I hope to find someone who wants to know me for the person I am in real life rather than the bloke they've seen on stage. The Alfie Boe who jumps about on stage, singing in a loud voice, is a very different person from the Alfie Boe who you might find shopping in Tesco Express on Uxbridge Road. It's always refreshing to me when I meet someone who hasn't got a clue who I am.

I remember one woman saying to me, 'Oh, I didn't know you were a singer, and definitely not a famous one. I'll have to google you!'

That was quite comforting for a split second, until I

thought, *Oh no! Please don't google me! I've no idea what's going to come up.*

·   ·   ·

Writing this book, it felt good to go back over some of my best and happiest moments – the highs, I guess you'd call them. But for my own sake, I also needed to talk about the lows, and there have been quite a few of those in the last ten years. More than I would have ever imagined and certainly more than I would have hoped.

Often, when we break up with someone we love, there's a sense of loss that's something like a bereavement. We grieve the loss of that person, of that relationship, even though nobody has died. The difference is, when a loved one dies, it's out of our control. When a relationship ends, and we lose a loved one, there's a sense of failure and shame added into the mix. This is something I have to work against every day just to keep in a positive frame of mind.

While I was filming *Freeze the Fear*, one of the show's producers called me with a question.

'Alfie, would it be OK for us to use the footage of you opening your heart and being really honest about your struggles?'

I didn't really have to think too hard about it. If what I've been through could help or even inspire someone who was watching the show, of course, I'd want them to use it.

So here we are! Now I've written about my pain and the struggles I've had. I've put it all down on paper. It's been hard to read back at times, but the most important thing for me now is to recognise the positives among all the negatives. The jewels in the dirt. To grab them with both hands, dust them off and let them pull me onwards to a new storyboard, another tale. A better, happier one.

My dad always used to tell me, 'It'll be all right, Son.'

Words I've always held on to and will carry with me moving forward. The truth is, we can and do get through tough times. We find ways to move on because we have to. Talking about what I've gone through is one of the things that's really helped me. I know I'm going to feel much more positive and in a better place now I've got all this down, but there are so many other, much simpler ways of unburdening.

Never be afraid to reach out to friends and family or to ask for help. Know that there are people who are there for you and who care about you. We're not always strong enough to do everything by ourselves, so please share the load if you can.

Of course, I still have sadness inside me. I sometimes have a longing for what I had. In those moments, I have to remind myself that it wasn't meant to be. That's why things have changed. This, now, is where my life is going and where my personal journey lies. Moving forward and not dwelling on the past is vital for all of us.

During a tough spell, having routines is one of the things that really helps me. You'd be amazed at the positive effect something as simple as making your bed when you get up each morning can have when you feel down. Or tidying your room or your house or even a wardrobe. If you have pride in your appearance and your surroundings, you start to have pride in yourself again. It's much easier to take on various challenges and worries when you have a positive mindset and feel good about yourself. Self-love and self-care are important tools to have in your bag.

The constant for me is and always has been music. It's my magic. I've sometimes used it to mask the pain or divert it, but I've also used it to help me connect with that pain and to sit with it when I need to. Music is the thing that's got me through, whether it's recording, performing on stage, writing songs or just singing in the shower. In many ways, it's my therapy.

It doesn't have to be music, though. Your thing might be sport or craft or travel or friends or any number of things. It doesn't matter what it is, the important thing is to make that joy a priority. Allow yourself time to do the things you love.

We need that joy in our lives, something that lifts us up and keeps us going.

I hope you all find your thing, your magic, and if you're not sure what it is yet, that's OK; you'll find it when the time is right for you. Eventually, you will start to grow and feel stronger.

I believe life should be lived to the full and in your own way, and love should be shared. Whatever it is you're looking for, I know you will find it.

Like my dad always said, 'It will be all right!'

ACKNOWLEDGEMENTS

A huge thank you to my amazing management team LME Worldwide – Craig Logan, Vikki Josephs and Lewis Shaw. Thank you for everything you do!

To the wonderful team at Ebury, thank you so much for giving me the opportunity to tell my story and share my experiences in my own words. Thanks to my editorial team – Ru Merritt, Jasmin Kaur and Zoë Jellicoe – as well as Lucy Brown and Nat Goncalves for your publicity and marketing expertise. Thanks also to Jamie Groves and David Bamford for your guidance throughout. To Sebastian Davey and Simon Long at Russells, a big thank you for helping, as always, with the legal side of things and thank you to my accountants Brian and Elizabeth. Thanks to Pål Hansen for a great photoshoot, Gemma Sheppard for the styling, Sadaf Ahmad for grooming and to Lisa Brewster for pulling the design together.

To my children, Gracie and Alfie. I love you so much and this book includes the beautiful memories and love we've shared over the years. Thank you for being my strength to carry on. To Sarah, we may have gone our separate ways, but the memories we shared will always be close to my heart.

Finally, a massive thank you to each and every one of you

reading my book – you are truly amazing and your continued support through everything I do is something I never take for granted. I wouldn't be here without you all and so I hope you enjoy this book!

Love,
Alfie